Assertive Comı
Complete Self-/

The guidance in thi: ... Community
Treatment best practices and standards in business process architecture, design and quality management. The guidance is also based on the professional judgment of the individual collaborators listed in the Acknowledgments.

Notice of rights

You are licensed to use the Self-Assessment contents in your presentations and materials for internal use and customers without asking us - we are here to help.

Trademarks

http://theartofservice.com
service@theartofservice.com

Table of Contents

About The Art of Service

The Art of Service, Business Process Architects since 2000, is dedicated to helping stakeholders achieve excellence.

Defining, designing, creating, and implementing a process to solve a stakeholders challenge or meet an objective is the most valuable role... In EVERY group, company, organization and department.

Unless you're talking a one-time, single-use project, there should be a process. Whether that process is managed and implemented by humans, AI, or a combination of the two, it needs to be designed by someone with a complex enough perspective to ask the right questions.

Someone capable of asking the right questions and step back and say, 'What are we really trying to accomplish here? And is there a different way to look at it?'

With The Art of Service's Standard Requirements Self-Assessments, we empower people who can do just that — whether their title is marketer, entrepreneur, manager, salesperson, consultant, Business Process Manager, executive assistant, IT Manager, CIO etc... —they are the people who rule the future. They are people who watch the process as it happens, and ask the right questions to make the process work better.

Contact us when you need any support with this Self-Assessment and any help with templates, blue-prints and examples of standard documents you might need:

http://theartofservice.com
service@theartofservice.com

Included Resources - how to access

Included with your purchase of the book is the Assertive

Community Treatment Self-Assessment Spreadsheet Dashboard which contains all questions and Self-Assessment areas and auto-generates insights, graphs, and project RACI planning - all with examples to get you started right away.

How? Simply send an email to
access@theartofservice.com
with this books' title in the subject to get the Assertive Community Treatment Self Assessment Tool right away.

You will receive the following contents with New and Updated specific criteria:

- The latest quick edition of the book in PDF
- The latest complete edition of the book in PDF, which criteria correspond to the criteria in...
- The Self-Assessment Excel Dashboard, and...
- Example pre-filled Self-Assessment Excel Dashboard to get familiar with results generation
- In-depth specific Checklists covering the topic
- Project management checklists and templates to assist with implementation

INCLUDES LIFETIME SELF ASSESSMENT UPDATES

Every self assessment comes with Lifetime Updates and Lifetime Free Updated Books. Lifetime Updates is an industry-first feature which allows you to receive verified self assessment updates, ensuring you always have the most accurate information at your fingertips.

Get it now- you will be glad you did - do it now, before you forget.

Send an email to **access@theartofservice.com** with this books' title in the subject to get the Assertive Community Treatment Self Assessment Tool right away.

Purpose of this Self-Assessment

This Self-Assessment has been developed to improve understanding of the requirements and elements of Assertive Community Treatment, based on best practices and standards in business process architecture, design and quality management.

It is designed to allow for a rapid Self-Assessment to determine how closely existing management practices and procedures correspond to the elements of the Self-Assessment.

The criteria of requirements and elements of Assertive Community Treatment have been rephrased in the format of a Self-Assessment questionnaire, with a seven-criterion scoring system, as explained in this document.

In this format, even with limited background knowledge of Assertive Community Treatment, a manager can quickly review existing operations to determine how they measure up to the standards. This in turn can serve as the starting point of a 'gap analysis' to identify management tools or system elements that might usefully be implemented in the organization to help improve overall performance.

How to use the Self-Assessment

On the following pages are a series of questions to identify to what extent your Assertive Community Treatment initiative is complete in comparison to the requirements set in standards.

To facilitate answering the questions, there is a space in front of each question to enter a score on a scale of '1' to '5'.

1 Strongly Disagree

2 Disagree

3 Neutral

4 Agree

5 Strongly Agree

Read the question and rate it with the following in front of mind:

'In my belief,
the answer to this question is clearly defined'.

There are two ways in which you can choose to interpret this statement;

1. how aware are you that the answer to the question is clearly defined
2. for more in-depth analysis you can choose to gather evidence and confirm the answer to the question. This obviously will take more time, most Self-Assessment users opt for the first way to interpret the question and dig deeper later on based on the outcome of the overall Self-Assessment.

A score of '1' would mean that the answer is not clear at all, where a '5' would mean the answer is crystal clear and defined. Leave emtpy when the question is not applicable or you don't want to answer it, you can skip it without affecting your score. Write your score in the space provided.

After you have responded to all the appropriate statements in each section, compute your average score for that section, using the formula provided, and round to the nearest tenth. Then transfer to the corresponding spoke in the Assertive Community Treatment Scorecard on the second next page of the Self-Assessment.

Your completed Assertive Community Treatment Scorecard will give you a clear presentation of which Assertive Community Treatment areas need attention.

Assertive Community Treatment Scorecard Example

Example of how the finalized Scorecard can look like:

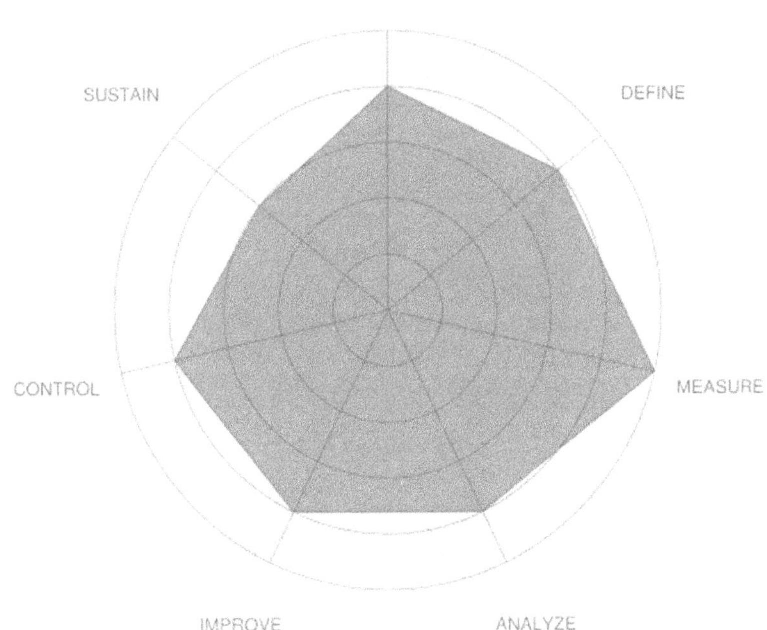

Assertive Community Treatment Scorecard

Your Scores:

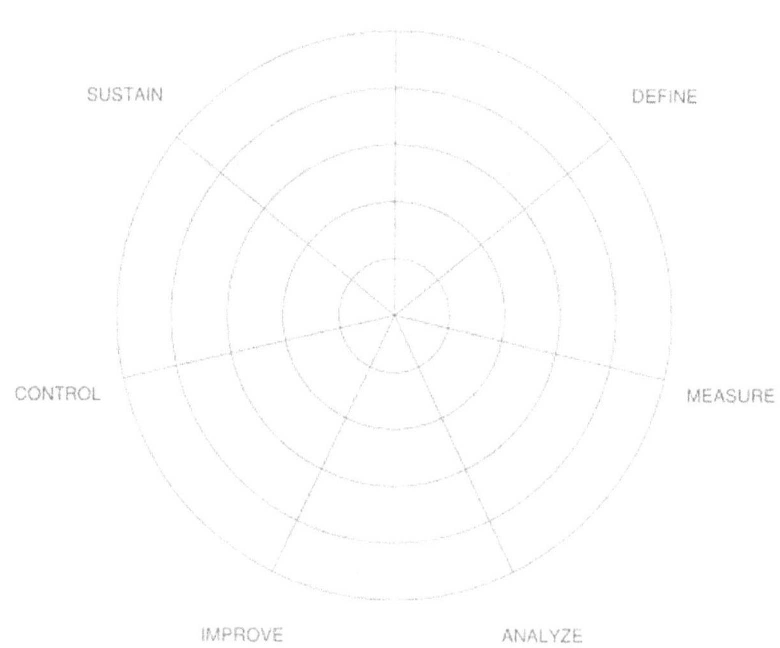

BEGINNING OF THE SELF-ASSESSMENT:

CRITERION #1: RECOGNIZE

INTENT: Be aware of the need for change. Recognize that there is an unfavorable variation, problem or symptom.

In my belief, the answer to this question is clearly defined:

5 Strongly Agree

4 Agree

3 Neutral

2 Disagree

1 Strongly Disagree

1. How often do you need to reassess the clients case management needs?
<--- Score

2. How do the range and availability of services meet user/carer needs?
<--- Score

3. How are you going to measure success?

<--- Score

4. Does the individual/family really need this assistance from a specialty mental health provider?
<--- Score

5. What are the expected benefits of Assertive Community Treatment to the stakeholder?
<--- Score

6. What are the key elements of a successful expression of continued need for services?
<--- Score

7. How do the goals and strategies of the program aim to solve the problem?
<--- Score

8. Are you seeing any trends in the way employers are handling mental heath issues?
<--- Score

9. How will the persons basic needs for food, shelter, and clothing be met outside the jail?
<--- Score

10. What are the major problems of mental world services?
<--- Score

11. How important is this in relation to other issues as resources and speed of access?
<--- Score

12. How would you rate the clients need for

psychiatric/psychological treatment?
<--- Score

13. Is there a technical-assistance organization in your state (or otherwise available) to help you address implementation concerns identified in earlier questions?
<--- Score

14. Addressing the social needs of mental health consumers when day treatment programs convert to supported employment: can consumer-run services play a role?
<--- Score

15. How are the Assertive Community Treatment's objectives aligned to the group's overall stakeholder strategy?
<--- Score

16. Are there any specific expectations or concerns about the Assertive Community Treatment team, Assertive Community Treatment itself?
<--- Score

17. As a sponsor, customer or management, how important is it to meet goals, objectives?
<--- Score

18. What does Assertive Community Treatment success mean to the stakeholders?
<--- Score

19. What services need to be offered by dental, mental and behavioral health sites?
<--- Score

20. What are the information needs of people seeking to self-care or live successfully with long-term physical and mental health conditions and what support do they need to use that information?
<--- Score

21. What other programs and services are needed in your community for substance abuse prevention and treatment?
<--- Score

22. What level of service is needed?
<--- Score

23. How often are participants required to meet with mental health program staff that performs case management to review progress, status of treatment, and ongoing needs during the last phase?
<--- Score

24. Does your program offer peer support services from people who have had mental health problems?
<--- Score

25. Do you need a referral for this?
<--- Score

26. Do you work with clients with mental health issues (or have you in the past)?
<--- Score

27. What problems might ACT solve for your

organization, community, and/or funder?
<--- Score

28. Combined severe mental health and substance use problems: What are the training and support needs of staff working with this client group?
<--- Score

29. How much are sponsors, customers, partners, stakeholders involved in Assertive Community Treatment? In other words, what are the risks, if Assertive Community Treatment does not deliver successfully?
<--- Score

30. What percentage of the identified clients will have Medicaid?
<--- Score

31. How many assertive community treatment teams do you need?
<--- Score

32. Does the client need additional services or interventions to be able to continue making progress?
<--- Score

33. Home confinement, or house arrest, is a community-based program Shelter care is an alternative that offers nonsecure residential care for youths who need it?
<--- Score

34. What kind of event prompts a referral to your program?

<--- Score

35. What do you need to know about medical necessity?
<--- Score

36. How specific will the protocols need to be for your organization/practices staff?
<--- Score

37. Does the mental model of the manager and the team need to be congruent?
<--- Score

38. What are the stakeholder objectives to be achieved with Assertive Community Treatment?
<--- Score

39. What, if any, resources are needed?
<--- Score

40. Are issues of special populations addressed (mentally ill)?
<--- Score

41. What resources will one need?
<--- Score

42. What is the treatment model used to treat clients with substance abuse problems?
<--- Score

43. What evidence is there that CTOs prevent dangerousness and get people the treatment they need?
<--- Score

44. What are you doing to assist employees in trying to pick out the already stated who might be having mental issues?
<--- Score

45. What supervisory structure and/or supervisory resources are needed to build an effective ACT team?
<--- Score

46. Is homelessness a mental health problem?
<--- Score

47. Are there any gaps in services needed by your clients?
<--- Score

48. What are the current barriers/ challenges to providing/accessing needed services?
<--- Score

49. What problems are present and under which circumstances do they emerge?
<--- Score

50. What problems are you facing and how do you consider Assertive Community Treatment will circumvent those obstacles?
<--- Score

51. What situation(s) led to this Assertive Community Treatment Self Assessment?
<--- Score

52. Are there issues with coordination across

services?
<--- Score

53. What needs do you foresee for staffing, resources, and resource intensity?
<--- Score

54. What services do not need a referral?
<--- Score

55. What needs assessment instrument do you use?
<--- Score

56. What roles need to be added to complete the ACT team?
<--- Score

57. What action will need to be taken, based on the measurement of the indicator?
<--- Score

58. How many forensic assertive community treatment teams do you need?
<--- Score

59. Why do you need what you need?
<--- Score

60. Has a formal assessment been conducted to explore the need for and viability?
<--- Score

61. What are the liability issues as a psychiatric consultant?
<--- Score

62. Who else hopes to benefit from it?
<--- Score

63. How is program set up to serve wide range of ages/needs?
<--- Score

64. When have you been on a team that needed to have a shared mental model?
<--- Score

65. What would happen if Assertive Community Treatment weren't done?
<--- Score

66. How many hours of work experience do you need?
<--- Score

Add up total points for this section:
_____ = Total points for this section

Divided by: ______ (number of statements answered) = ______
Average score for this section

Transfer your score to the Assertive Community Treatment Index at the beginning of the Self-Assessment.

CRITERION #2: DEFINE:

INTENT: Formulate the stakeholder problem. Define the problem, needs and objectives.

In my belief, the answer to this question is clearly defined:

5 Strongly Agree

4 Agree

3 Neutral

2 Disagree

1 Strongly Disagree

1. What constraints exist that might impact the team?
<--- Score

2. Has anyone else (internal or external to the group) attempted to solve this problem or a similar one before? If so, what knowledge can be leveraged from these previous efforts?
<--- Score

3. What critical content must be communicated – who, what, when, where, and how?
<--- Score

4. Do you intend to remain involved with the applicant if he/she secures case management services?
<--- Score

5. What specifically is the problem? Where does it occur? When does it occur? What is its extent?
<--- Score

6. What are the dynamics of the communication plan?
<--- Score

7. Will you be required to list supportive employment, employment assistant, and targeted case management providers in your provider directory?
<--- Score

8. Will your staff talk frequently with your case manager or psychiatrist if you ask them to?
<--- Score

9. Does the team have regular meetings?
<--- Score

10. Are activities considered billable under Case Management - Transition Linkage and Aftercare?
<--- Score

11. How was the 'as is' process map developed, reviewed, verified and validated?
<--- Score

12. Is the current 'as is' process being followed? If not, what are the discrepancies?
<--- Score

13. What is the maximum case load a case manager can be assigned?
<--- Score

14. What is it that makes a case a crisis?
<--- Score

15. How often are the team meetings?
<--- Score

16. How does the case management for long-term mentally ill individuals affect use of health care services?
<--- Score

17. Why are good case notes so important?
<--- Score

18. Can case management be taught in a multidisciplinary forum?
<--- Score

19. Is there a unique billing code for case management, collateral contact?
<--- Score

20. What factors does the team consider when closing a case?
<--- Score

21. Is the improvement team aware of the different

versions of a process: what they think it is vs. what it actually is vs. what it should be vs. what it could be?
<--- Score

22. Does the rule address who may provide case management services?
<--- Score

23. Have you met the person receiving services case manager/service coordinator?
<--- Score

24. What customer feedback methods were used to solicit their input?
<--- Score

25. Does your organization provide case management services to the elderly?
<--- Score

26. What makes case management work for people experiencing homelessness?
<--- Score

27. What factors affect the efficacy of intensive case management in reducing rates of organization re-admission for people with severe mental health illness?
<--- Score

28. How will the Assertive Community Treatment team and the group measure complete success of Assertive Community Treatment?
<--- Score

29. Has the direction changed at all during the course

of Assertive Community Treatment? If so, when did it change and why?
<--- Score

30. Why have case management services been recommended and implemented so frequently in the area of homelessness?
<--- Score

31. Who provides assertive case management?
<--- Score

32. What are the requirements for accessing services?
<--- Score

33. Who is providing case management services?
<--- Score

34. Has a team charter been developed and communicated?
<--- Score

35. Where do most of your clients live and how does case management get them up the ladder?
<--- Score

36. How often are participants required to attend mental health program sessions during the last phase?
<--- Score

37. When is the estimated completion date?
<--- Score

38. Are there different segments of customers?

<--- Score

39. Did the client attend the case conference?
<--- Score

40. Who is paying for case management?
<--- Score

41. In which way could your work benefit from the introduction of case management?
<--- Score

42. Does the case manager apply case management on both levels, the case and system level?
<--- Score

43. Which employer will conduct the case management?
<--- Score

44. Are customers identified and high impact areas defined?
<--- Score

45. Are prior authorizations required to exceed limits on substance abuse treatment services?
<--- Score

46. Has the Assertive Community Treatment work been fairly and/or equitably divided and delegated among team members who are qualified and capable to perform the work? Has everyone contributed?
<--- Score

47. Is Assertive Community Treatment linked to key

stakeholder goals and objectives?
<--- Score

48. Is there a completed, verified, and validated high-level 'as is' (not 'should be' or 'could be') stakeholder process map?
<--- Score

49. Can case managers earn the required year of experience while on-the-job?
<--- Score

50. Which tasks does the case manager take over?
<--- Score

51. What is case management and what can it be used for?
<--- Score

52. What is your organizations requirement?
<--- Score

53. What is assertive case management?
<--- Score

54. When are meeting minutes sent out? Who is on the distribution list?
<--- Score

55. Have the customer needs been translated into specific, measurable requirements? How?
<--- Score

56. What level of support is required for compliance with medication regimen?
<--- Score

57. Can case management-transition linkage and aftercare services be used only while a person is in your organization, or just immediately after?
<--- Score

58. Are there any values that conflict with your values as a case manager?
<--- Score

59. Is a fully trained team formed, supported, and committed to work on the Assertive Community Treatment improvements?
<--- Score

60. Will team members perform Assertive Community Treatment work when assigned and in a timely fashion?
<--- Score

61. Will the lender require inspections and approvals of incremental draws?
<--- Score

62. Are customer(s) identified and segmented according to their different needs and requirements?
<--- Score

63. What are the rough order estimates on cost savings/opportunities that Assertive Community Treatment brings?
<--- Score

64. Is the team adequately staffed with the desired cross-functionality? If not, what additional resources are available to the team?

<--- Score

65. Has the improvement team collected the 'voice of the customer' (obtained feedback – qualitative and quantitative)?
<--- Score

66. Is the Assertive Community Treatment scope manageable?
<--- Score

67. Do you have a caseload of consumers?
<--- Score

68. What would be the goal or target for a Assertive Community Treatment's improvement team?
<--- Score

69. Is the team formed and are team leaders (Coaches and Management Leads) assigned?
<--- Score

70. Do the problem and goal statements meet the SMART criteria (specific, measurable, attainable, relevant, and time-bound)?
<--- Score

71. When is/was the Assertive Community Treatment start date?
<--- Score

72. Which functions and tasks does your organizations case manager have?
<--- Score

73. Is case management accomplishing its mission

and goals?
<--- Score

74. Are there any constraints known that bear on the ability to perform Assertive Community Treatment work? How is the team addressing them?
<--- Score

75. How will required services be provided?
<--- Score

76. Is the team equipped with available and reliable resources?
<--- Score

77. Are improvement team members fully trained on Assertive Community Treatment?
<--- Score

78. Are your mental health program program eligibility requirements written?
<--- Score

79. How does the Assertive Community Treatment manager ensure against scope creep?
<--- Score

80. Has everyone on the team, including the team leaders, been properly trained?
<--- Score

81. What are the components of case management?
<--- Score

82. What are the Roles and Responsibilities for each

team member and its leadership? Where is this documented?
<--- Score

83. Which changes are targeted from the point of views of the client, the case manager and third parties?
<--- Score

84. Are the requirements different for a case manager versus a case manager supervisor?
<--- Score

85. Have you reviewed the role of the integrated case manager of your team?
<--- Score

86. Are people receiving case management services satisfied with services?
<--- Score

87. Is there regularly 100% attendance at the team meetings? If not, have appointed substitutes attended to preserve cross-functionality and full representation?
<--- Score

88. Does the effectiveness of case management differ according to intervention characteristics?
<--- Score

89. What is the best case management model?
<--- Score

90. Is case management effective for people with serious mental illness?

<--- Score

91. What are the implications for staff workload and caseload?
<--- Score

92. Are stakeholder processes mapped?
<--- Score

93. Is the team sponsored by a champion or stakeholder leader?
<--- Score

94. What are the compelling stakeholder reasons for embarking on Assertive Community Treatment?
<--- Score

95. Will team members regularly document their Assertive Community Treatment work?
<--- Score

96. Will case management continue to include support services provided to help clients maintain access to services?
<--- Score

97. What is the active caseload for supervision officers on the mental health program team?
<--- Score

98. Is there a critical path to deliver Assertive Community Treatment results?
<--- Score

99. How will variation in the actual durations of each activity be dealt with to ensure that the expected

Assertive Community Treatment results are met?
<--- Score

100. What is the significance of quality in the context of case management?
<--- Score

101. Is data collected and displayed to better understand customer(s) critical needs and requirements.
<--- Score

102. How did the Assertive Community Treatment manager receive input to the development of a Assertive Community Treatment improvement plan and the estimated completion dates/times of each activity?
<--- Score

103. How often are participants required to attend mental health program sessions during phase 1?
<--- Score

104. Is there a completed SIPOC representation, describing the Suppliers, Inputs, Process, Outputs, and Customers?
<--- Score

105. Are facilities required to provide a minimum number of service/treatment hours to residents?
<--- Score

106. In the case of a treatment protocol, does it work or not?
<--- Score

107. Is there a mentality that considers lump-sum contracts just require delivery of deliverables?
<--- Score

108. Is there a Assertive Community Treatment management charter, including stakeholder case, problem and goal statements, scope, milestones, roles and responsibilities, communication plan?
<--- Score

109. How do you keep key subject matter experts in the loop?
<--- Score

110. Has a high-level 'as is' process map been completed, verified and validated?
<--- Score

111. How many clients can case manager have?
<--- Score

112. Has/have the customer(s) been identified?
<--- Score

113. What key stakeholder process output measure(s) does Assertive Community Treatment leverage and how?
<--- Score

114. What is required to make mental health promotion effective in the workplace?
<--- Score

115. What are the boundaries of the scope? What is in bounds and what is not? What is the start point? What is the stop point?

<--- Score

116. Who is providing case management?
<--- Score

117. Is Assertive Community Treatment currently on schedule according to the plan?
<--- Score

118. How is the team tracking and documenting its work?
<--- Score

119. Who are the Assertive Community Treatment improvement team members, including Management Leads and Coaches?
<--- Score

120. Does gap cover active case management as well?
<--- Score

121. How do case managers communicate to consumers that relationship is primary and essential?
<--- Score

122. Are there multiple case management models?
<--- Score

123. Are team charters developed?
<--- Score

124. If substitutes have been appointed, have they been briefed on the Assertive Community Treatment goals and received regular communications as to the

progress to date?
<--- Score

125. Has a project plan, Gantt chart, or similar been developed/completed?
<--- Score

126. Does your organization have the necessary premises, e time resources, suitable instruments and the working material in order to conduct case management?
<--- Score

127. Which objectives do you pursue with the introduction of case management?
<--- Score

128. Is full participation by members in regularly held team meetings guaranteed?
<--- Score

129. If participants are found to have co-occurring disorders, is substance abuse treatment required as part of mental health court-related treatment?
<--- Score

130. Are different versions of process maps needed to account for the different types of inputs?
<--- Score

Add up total points for this section:
_____ = Total points for this section

Divided by: ______ (number of statements answered) = ______
Average score for this section

Transfer your score to the Assertive Community Treatment Index at the beginning of the Self-Assessment.

CRITERION #3: MEASURE:

INTENT: Gather the correct data. Measure the current performance and evolution of the situation.

In my belief, the answer to this question is clearly defined:

5 Strongly Agree

4 Agree

3 Neutral

2 Disagree

1 Strongly Disagree

1. Is data collected on key measures that were identified?
<--- Score

2. Is a solid data collection plan established that includes measurement systems analysis?
<--- Score

3. Is data collection planned and executed?

<--- Score

4. Does your organization/practice assure that treatment objective measures are being collected?
<--- Score

5. What are the most cost-effective methods for training/re-skilling professional staff for community work?
<--- Score

6. What are critical root mental skills that build and develop the leader capacities that are essential for extraordinary performance in extreme conditions?
<--- Score

7. How large is the gap between current performance and the customer-specified (goal) performance?
<--- Score

8. Are process variation components displayed/ communicated using suitable charts, graphs, plots?
<--- Score

9. What is the timing of payments relative to implementation - cash flowing the cost of hiring team?
<--- Score

10. Is long term and short term variability accounted for?
<--- Score

11. Are key measures identified and agreed upon?
<--- Score

12. Is there a Performance Baseline?
<--- Score

13. If there are mental processes that impact maintainability, what is measured for them?
<--- Score

14. Which sources have you ever used to obtain information for environmental scanning analysis?
<--- Score

15. Is Process Variation Displayed/Communicated?
<--- Score

16. What are the costs of effective treatment?
<--- Score

17. What data was collected (past, present, future/ongoing)?
<--- Score

18. Does your organization consider the potential impact of risks on industry and the community?
<--- Score

19. What are the key input variables? What are the key process variables? What are the key output variables?
<--- Score

20. Was a data collection plan established?
<--- Score

21. What particular quality tools did the team find helpful in establishing measurements?
<--- Score

22. Does the clients individual mental and/or physical capacity, understanding of potential risks or communication skills affect the impact of the incident?
<--- Score

23. How does this impact on client-centered care for people with schizophrenia?
<--- Score

24. What key measures identified indicate the performance of the stakeholder process?
<--- Score

25. Does stress cause psychiatric illness?
<--- Score

26. How does the Assertive Community Treatment program affect utilization-based measures of quality?
<--- Score

27. What are the agreed upon definitions of the high impact areas, defect(s), unit(s), and opportunities that will figure into the process capability metrics?
<--- Score

28. Have you found any 'ground fruit' or 'low-hanging fruit' for immediate remedies to the gap in performance?
<--- Score

29. Are high impact defects defined and identified in the stakeholder process?
<--- Score

30. Have you conducted a comprehensive process analysis and inventory of services?
<--- Score

31. Does case management matter as your organization cost-control strategy?
<--- Score

32. How do you determine impact of social support on the service user?
<--- Score

33. Who participated in the data collection for measurements?
<--- Score

34. How will you measure progress?
<--- Score

35. What has the team done to assure the stability and accuracy of the measurement process?
<--- Score

36. How can a mental cause give rise to a behavioral effect that has a position in space?
<--- Score

37. Is your organization/practice a cost-based entity?
<--- Score

38. What impact does the ACT program have on member health care experience?
<--- Score

39. What impact does the ACT program have on

overall cost of care for individuals?
<--- Score

40. Is key measure data collection planned and executed, process variation displayed and communicated and performance baselined?
<--- Score

41. What charts has the team used to display the components of variation in the process?
<--- Score

Add up total points for this section:
_____ = Total points for this section

Divided by: ______ (number of statements answered) = ______
Average score for this section

Transfer your score to the Assertive Community Treatment Index at the beginning of the Self-Assessment.

CRITERION #4: ANALYZE:

INTENT: Analyze causes, assumptions and hypotheses.

In my belief, the answer to this question is clearly defined:

5 Strongly Agree

4 Agree

3 Neutral

2 Disagree

1 Strongly Disagree

1. What process or methods did you use to conduct a participatory program evaluation?
<--- Score

2. Does the case belong in the realm of a Case Management process?
<--- Score

3. Is the Assertive Community Treatment process severely broken such that a re-design is necessary?

<--- Score

4. Have all non-recommended alternatives been analyzed in sufficient detail?
<--- Score

5. What are the revised rough estimates of the financial savings/opportunity for Assertive Community Treatment improvements?
<--- Score

6. What were the crucial 'moments of truth' on the process map?
<--- Score

7. Who is responsible for which parts of the application process?
<--- Score

8. Which changes occurred during the case management process?
<--- Score

9. What tools were used to narrow the list of possible causes?
<--- Score

10. Are the tools that are used validated, and do screening processes have the capacity to identify cognitive, behavioural, mental and physical conditions, issues or risks of harm?
<--- Score

11. How was the detailed process map generated, verified, and validated?
<--- Score

12. How will the case management process be evaluated?
<--- Score

13. Was a cause-and-effect diagram used to explore the different types of causes (or sources of variation)?
<--- Score

14. Is conscious awareness a required prerequisite for mental processes?
<--- Score

15. Do staff have the necessary skills to collect, analyze, and report data?
<--- Score

16. How will required elements be handled within your organization/practice processes?
<--- Score

17. What does the data say about the performance of the stakeholder process?
<--- Score

18. How does the ACT referral process through the Single Point of Access (SPOA) system work?
<--- Score

19. What tools were used to generate the list of possible causes?
<--- Score

20. Is data and process analysis, root cause analysis and quantifying the gap/opportunity in place?
<--- Score

21. What is the cost of poor quality as supported by the team's analysis?
<--- Score

22. Which stakeholder characteristics are analyzed?
<--- Score

23. What is your role in the process?
<--- Score

24. Have the problem and goal statements been updated to reflect the additional knowledge gained from the analyze phase?
<--- Score

25. What quality tools were used to get through the analyze phase?
<--- Score

26. What are the techniques that you use during the engagement process?
<--- Score

27. Did any additional data need to be collected?
<--- Score

28. Does Assertive Community Treatment systematically track and analyze outcomes for accountability and quality improvement?
<--- Score

29. Have changes been properly/adequately analyzed for effect?
<--- Score

30. How long will it take to process a complaint?
<--- Score

31. What are the major components and processes involved in your case management models?
<--- Score

32. What is the general content and process of a session?
<--- Score

33. What do you have in terms of data?
<--- Score

34. What conclusions were drawn from the team's data collection and analysis? How did the team reach these conclusions?
<--- Score

35. Does your organization systematically track and analyze outcomes related for accountability and quality improvement?
<--- Score

36. Which qualifications and skills should case managers have, and what type of support should be provided?
<--- Score

37. Have any additional benefits been identified that will result from closing all or most of the gaps?
<--- Score

38. Did any value-added analysis or 'lean thinking' take place to identify some of the gaps shown on the

'as is' process map?
<--- Score

39. What are your key Assertive Community Treatment indicators that you will measure, analyze and track?
<--- Score

40. Are losses documented, analyzed, and remedial processes developed to prevent future losses?
<--- Score

41. Was a detailed process map created to amplify critical steps of the 'as is' stakeholder process?
<--- Score

42. What mental models are necessary to help auditors build knowledge structures that will allow them to more effectively process and evaluate more complex data?
<--- Score

43. How will processes during the case management be recorded?
<--- Score

44. Does your service have criteria or a process for triaging people who are referred?
<--- Score

45. What did the team gain from developing a sub-process map?
<--- Score

46. Were any designed experiments used to generate

additional insight into the data analysis?
<--- Score

47. Were Pareto charts (or similar) used to portray the 'heavy hitters' (or key sources of variation)?
<--- Score

48. Are stakeholders involved in the development process?
<--- Score

49. Have the types of risks that may impact Assertive Community Treatment been identified and analyzed?
<--- Score

50. What were the financial benefits resulting from any 'ground fruit or low-hanging fruit' (quick fixes)?
<--- Score

51. Have the concerns of stakeholders to help identify and define potential barriers been obtained and analyzed?
<--- Score

52. Is the performance gap determined?
<--- Score

53. Which changes did occur by the end of the case management process?
<--- Score

54. What are the qualifications of staff who work in the program?
<--- Score

55. How do you identify and analyze stakeholders and their interests?
<--- Score

56. How will the Assertive Community Treatment data be analyzed?
<--- Score

57. Are gaps between current performance and the goal performance identified?
<--- Score

58. Does your organization/practice benchmark the results of any of your data collection efforts?
<--- Score

59. Is the gap/opportunity displayed and communicated in financial terms?
<--- Score

60. Do you evaluate your processes regularly?
<--- Score

61. Is there a process for transfer of cases between shelter ACT teams when residents move, or can that be considered?
<--- Score

62. Were there any improvement opportunities identified from the process analysis?
<--- Score

63. Do the electronic program data include information from the treatment provider?
<--- Score

64. Are pertinent alerts monitored, analyzed and distributed to appropriate personnel?
<--- Score

65. Who is responsible for the whole case management process?
<--- Score

Add up total points for this section:
_____ = Total points for this section

Divided by: ______ (number of statements answered) = ______
Average score for this section

Transfer your score to the Assertive Community Treatment Index at the beginning of the Self-Assessment.

CRITERION #5: IMPROVE:

INTENT: Develop a practical solution. Innovate, establish and test the solution and to measure the results.

In my belief, the answer to this question is clearly defined:

5 Strongly Agree

4 Agree

3 Neutral

2 Disagree

1 Strongly Disagree

1. What were the underlying assumptions on the cost-benefit analysis?
<--- Score

2. What have been the results of studies completed to date?
<--- Score

3. How does the solution remove the key sources of

issues discovered in the analyze phase?
<--- Score

4. Did you have a clear understanding of your role and responsibilities?
<--- Score

5. How do you improve the effectiveness of Assertive Community Treatment?
<--- Score

6. How will the team or the process owner(s) monitor the implementation plan to see that it is working as intended?
<--- Score

7. What changes do you make that can lead to an improvement?
<--- Score

8. Do cognitive improvements have an effect on real-life functioning?
<--- Score

9. Is the user informed in case of risks on human mental integrity (nudging) by the product?
<--- Score

10. What is Assertive Community Treatment's impact on utilizing the best solution(s)?
<--- Score

11. Was a pilot designed for the proposed solution(s)?
<--- Score

12. When does teamwork translate into improved

team performance?
<--- Score

13. How do you develop new tools, skills, knowledge and mental models to understand privacy issues and take control of your personal information?
<--- Score

14. Are possible solutions generated and tested?
<--- Score

15. Why was members assertive positive solutions (maps) / assertive community treatment (ACT) created?
<--- Score

16. Does mental association or link between the earlier trademark and the later trademark automatically result in detriment to the earlier trademarks repute or distinctive character?
<--- Score

17. What is necessary to enhance development and utilization of treatment?
<--- Score

18. What documents do you need to submit with an online application?
<--- Score

19. What is the implementation plan?
<--- Score

20. What tools were most useful during the improve phase?

<--- Score

21. Do you develop an ACT program with a targeted time frame for service delivery that is driven by personal goal achievement?
<--- Score

22. Adding consumer-providers to intensive case management: does it improve outcome?
<--- Score

23. What tools were used to tap into the creativity and encourage 'outside the box' thinking?
<--- Score

24. Were any criteria developed to assist the team in testing and evaluating potential solutions?
<--- Score

25. How does this apply to people who have not been identified as being at high risk of deterioration in mental state?
<--- Score

26. How do you document your training?
<--- Score

27. What tools were used to evaluate the potential solutions?
<--- Score

28. Will you be able to interpret the results easily?
<--- Score

29. Are improved process ('should be') maps modified based on pilot data and analysis?

<--- Score

30. Do/does the probation/supervision officer(s) have low-risk clients as part of the caseload?
<--- Score

31. Did the executive board make a decision regarding the introduction of case management?
<--- Score

32. Describe the design of the pilot and what tests were conducted, if any?
<--- Score

33. Is a contingency plan established?
<--- Score

34. How do you document your work experience?
<--- Score

35. How will the group know that the solution worked?
<--- Score

36. What does the 'should be' process map/design look like?
<--- Score

37. How should case work practice develop in the context of multidisciplinary working?
<--- Score

38. Have you ever been diagnosed with a physical condition or mental health disorder involving potential health risk to the public?
<--- Score

39. What is the current understanding by the shelters on how they will work with the ACT teams?
<--- Score

40. Is there a small-scale pilot for proposed improvement(s)? What conclusions were drawn from the outcomes of a pilot?
<--- Score

41. How do the mental skills interact to best develop the leader capacities?
<--- Score

42. How can services be evaluated both quantitatively and qualitatively?
<--- Score

43. Is pilot data collected and analyzed?
<--- Score

44. What level of risk do you accept?
<--- Score

45. Are new and improved process ('should be') maps developed?
<--- Score

46. Does the scenario connect directly to the mental maps and concerns of users?
<--- Score

47. User involvement in mental health service development: how far can it go?
<--- Score

48. Does improvement depend on the magnitude of the impairment?
<--- Score

49. Is the optimal solution selected based on testing and analysis?
<--- Score

50. Improving the physical health-mental health interface for the chronically mentally ill: could nurse case managers make a difference?
<--- Score

51. Is a solution implementation plan established, including schedule/work breakdown structure, resources, risk management plan, cost/budget, and control plan?
<--- Score

52. Are there any constraints (technical, political, cultural, or otherwise) that would inhibit certain solutions?
<--- Score

53. How did the team generate the list of possible solutions?
<--- Score

54. Is there an improvement of substance abuse problems over time?
<--- Score

55. How can new technologies be used to improve quality in mental health practice?
<--- Score

56. Does team training improve team performance?
<--- Score

57. Does assertive community outreach improve social support?
<--- Score

58. What program or service were you evaluating?
<--- Score

59. Is the implementation plan designed?
<--- Score

60. What lessons, if any, from a pilot were incorporated into the design of the full-scale solution?
<--- Score

61. Have you had an outside evaluator measure whether the mental health program is achieving its intended outcomes?
<--- Score

62. Have you had an outside evaluator measure whether the mental health program is being implemented as intended?
<--- Score

63. Are there factors that indicate a level of uncertainty in this risk assessment?
<--- Score

64. Does interactive television improve mental engagement with program and advertising content?

<--- Score

65. What error proofing will be done to address some of the discrepancies observed in the 'as is' process?
<--- Score

66. What sequential combination of services produces the best results?
<--- Score

67. Quality improvement, pay for performance, and outcomes measurement: what makes sense?
<--- Score

68. Are the best solutions selected?
<--- Score

69. Which techniques are helpful to better understand the mental model behind FaaS?
<--- Score

70. What attendant changes will need to be made to ensure that the solution is successful?
<--- Score

71. What communications are necessary to support the implementation of the solution?
<--- Score

72. What are the key negative results with customers, clients and employees?
<--- Score

73. Is there a cost/benefit analysis of optimal solution(s)?
<--- Score

74. What is the team's contingency plan for potential problems occurring in implementation?
<--- Score

75. Do comprehensive performance measurement systems help or hinder managers mental model development?
<--- Score

76. Do addicted and mentally ill persons have the capacity to make autonomous decisions regarding treatment?
<--- Score

77. Is the adoption of environmental practices a strategical decision for small service companies?
<--- Score

78. How do you evaluate a mental revolution?
<--- Score

79. Is the level of psychosocial problems associated with improvements on delinquency outcomes?
<--- Score

80. Do you really have a clear vision and risk mentality?
<--- Score

81. Does animation help users build mental maps of spatial information?
<--- Score

82. How do you recognize continuous quality

improvement?
<--- Score

83. When to refer for further psychiatric evaluation or more restrictive treatment?
<--- Score

Add up total points for this section:
_____ = Total points for this section

Divided by: ______ (number of statements answered) = ______ Average score for this section

Transfer your score to the Assertive Community Treatment Index at the beginning of the Self-Assessment.

CRITERION #6: CONTROL:

INTENT: Implement the practical solution. Maintain the performance and correct possible complications.

In my belief, the answer to this question is clearly defined:

5 Strongly Agree

4 Agree

3 Neutral

2 Disagree

1 Strongly Disagree

1. How will the process owner verify improvement in present and future sigma levels, process capabilities?
<--- Score

2. What are the critical parameters to watch?
<--- Score

3. What types of assessments relate to career planning?

<--- Score

4. Do people understand that they can request that a person-centered planning meeting be convened whenever they want, and that they are not restricted to a once a year event?
<--- Score

5. Will meeting the plans interventions give the client the ability to live in the community?
<--- Score

6. Is the client working toward meeting goal(s) established in the treatment plan?
<--- Score

7. What did you learn that you did not know before?
<--- Score

8. Do all participants understand respective responsibilities in implementing the plan?
<--- Score

9. Is there a recommended audit plan for routine surveillance inspections of Assertive Community Treatment's gains?
<--- Score

10. Are the plans objectives appropriate to the clients current needs, skills, and abilities?
<--- Score

11. Are managed care clients experiencing shorter organization stays and does this raise concerns about quality of care under corresponding plans?

<--- Score

12. How does team learning lead to the development of shared mental models?
<--- Score

13. How do staff that are responsible for social work monitor the residents progress in improving physical, mental and psychosocial functioning?
<--- Score

14. If you use a risk assessment tool, has it been validated and standardized for your program population?
<--- Score

15. Will any special training be provided for results interpretation?
<--- Score

16. What does a treatment plan look like?
<--- Score

17. How will the day-to-day responsibilities for monitoring and continual improvement be transferred from the improvement team to the process owner?
<--- Score

18. Do you monitor the information you collect on program participants to asses whether the mental health is moving toward its goals?
<--- Score

19. Have updated plans been shared with all team members?

<--- Score

20. What is evidence for and against the quote?
<--- Score

21. How will new or emerging customer needs/ requirements be checked/communicated to orient the process toward meeting the new specifications and continually reducing variation?
<--- Score

22. Do team learning processes predict the temporal trajectory of team performance?
<--- Score

23. How is manager/leader standard work different?
<--- Score

24. What is manager/leader standard work?
<--- Score

25. Are the services provided to the client meeting the objectives of the service plan?
<--- Score

26. Does the purchase directly relate to identified needs outlined in the members recovery plan?
<--- Score

27. Does the date of the annual review need to be the same as the effective date of the treatment plan, or before it?
<--- Score

28. What key inputs and outputs are being measured

on an ongoing basis?
<--- Score

29. Does your organization/practice assure that the treatment plan objectives are followed?
<--- Score

30. What other areas of the group might benefit from the Assertive Community Treatment team's improvements, knowledge, and learning?
<--- Score

31. Has your mental health program made adjustments in policy or practice based on monitoring?
<--- Score

32. Does the Assertive Community Treatment performance meet the customer's requirements?
<--- Score

33. Are services occurring at the amount, scope, and duration specified in the individual plan of service?
<--- Score

34. Is knowledge gained on process shared and institutionalized?
<--- Score

35. How can an agent learn new skills, both mental and physical?
<--- Score

36. What are the treatment standards?
<--- Score

37. What other systems, operations, processes, and infrastructures (hiring practices, staffing, training, incentives/rewards, metrics/dashboards/scorecards, etc.) need updates, additions, changes, or deletions in order to facilitate knowledge transfer and improvements?
<--- Score

38. Are documented procedures clear and easy to follow for the operators?
<--- Score

39. Does the mental health program and/or case manager develop a case management plan for each participant?
<--- Score

40. When should the treatment plan be changed?
<--- Score

41. Is there documentation that will support the successful operation of the improvement?
<--- Score

42. Are new process steps, standards, and documentation ingrained into normal operations?
<--- Score

43. Are you preparing for audit under the current standards without putting in place systems and processes for the revised standards?
<--- Score

44. Is a response plan established and deployed?
<--- Score

45. Are there common grounds for international forensic psychiatry and psychology standards?
<--- Score

46. Are staff members who collect specimens trained in standard collection protocols?
<--- Score

47. Have you made any current plans?
<--- Score

48. What activities occur in the monitoring phase of the service?
<--- Score

49. How will the process owner and team be able to hold the gains?
<--- Score

50. Do the clients understand the process that will be used to monitor and evaluate the plan over time?
<--- Score

51. How often must the individualized treatment/ service plans be updated?
<--- Score

52. What have you learned about stakeholder involvement in program evaluation?
<--- Score

53. Does a troubleshooting guide exist or is it needed?
<--- Score

54. Have new or revised work instructions resulted?
<--- Score

55. Is there a clear methodology for the planning and deployment of staffing that is firmly rooted in an evidence based approach?
<--- Score

56. If you use a needs assessment tool, has it been validated and standardized for your program population?
<--- Score

57. Does the case manager conduct the case management process by using the phase model and does he/she always pay attention to ethical standards?
<--- Score

58. What aspects of treatment helped/hindered post-psychotic adjustment?
<--- Score

59. How will input, process, and output variables be checked to detect for sub-optimal conditions?
<--- Score

60. What is the recommended frequency of auditing?
<--- Score

61. Is there a transfer of ownership and knowledge to process owner and process team tasked with the responsibilities.
<--- Score

62. Are operating procedures consistent?

<--- Score

63. What have you learned about optimal services delivery?
<--- Score

64. Is new knowledge gained imbedded in the response plan?
<--- Score

65. Is your organization committed to routine processes that monitor progress toward full implementation or other evidence-based practices?
<--- Score

66. Does team adaptation mediate the effect of team learning on team performance?
<--- Score

67. How does your organization involve ACT team members and other staff in outcomes development and monitoring?
<--- Score

68. Do temporal mental model similarity and accuracy interact in predicting team learning behaviors?
<--- Score

69. Are the clients actively involved in developing, monitoring and evaluating the plan?
<--- Score

70. Have adjustments in policy or practice in your mental health program been made based on

feedback from the outside evaluation?
<--- Score

71. Is the client getting the services established by the service plan?
<--- Score

72. Are facilities required to develop individualized treatment/service plans for residents?
<--- Score

73. Are there documented procedures?
<--- Score

74. What features of a Benefits Plan can support employees with mental health issues?
<--- Score

75. Is there a control plan in place for sustaining improvements (short and long-term)?
<--- Score

76. Does job training on the documented procedures need to be part of the process team's education and training?
<--- Score

77. Are any diet plans, diet aids, or diet programs recommended for your clients?
<--- Score

78. Who will provide follow up and review the plan?
<--- Score

79. What sources of funding and program or infrastructure changes does your plan involve?
<--- Score

80. Are suggested corrective/restorative actions indicated on the response plan for known causes to problems that might surface?
<--- Score

81. How might the group capture best practices and lessons learned so as to leverage improvements?
<--- Score

82. How will report readings be checked to effectively monitor performance?
<--- Score

83. Who is the Assertive Community Treatment process owner?
<--- Score

84. How do you plan to sustain funding for mental health in the future?
<--- Score

85. What accreditation standards will encourage high-quality ACT services?
<--- Score

86. Do you have marketing plans that target payers, referral sources, and the general public?
<--- Score

87. Do you have a plan for accessing the services of a psychiatrist(s)?
<--- Score

88. Do you have a say in what services are included in your treatment plan?
<--- Score

89. Is a response plan in place for when the input, process, or output measures indicate an 'out-of-control' condition?
<--- Score

90. What does it mean to have user participation in planning?
<--- Score

91. How well does your team know each others specialty of practice and how is that support reflected in treatment of clients?
<--- Score

92. What should the next improvement project be that is related to Assertive Community Treatment?
<--- Score

93. What do you want them to learn?
<--- Score

94. How are treatment plan elements prioritized?
<--- Score

95. Does the plan reflect the current situation of the clients?
<--- Score

96. Has the improved process and its steps been standardized?
<--- Score

97. Who usually initiates the development of care/ mental health care plans?
<--- Score

98. Is there evidence that the individuals desired participants were contacted for availability before the planning meeting date is scheduled?
<--- Score

99. Has it been evaluated, or are there plans in place to evaluate it?
<--- Score

100. Are you learning what you thought you would?
<--- Score

101. When does engaging in team learning processes benefit team performance improvement?
<--- Score

102. What is the evidence for and against the belief?
<--- Score

103. What is the control/monitoring plan?
<--- Score

104. Can the crisis Intervention Plan order services?
<--- Score

105. Is there a standardized process?
<--- Score

106. Does the response plan contain a definite closed loop continual improvement scheme (e.g., plan-do-check-act)?
<--- Score

107. Does a psychiatrist need to sign the service plan?
<--- Score

108. Is there still an interim treatment plan?
<--- Score

109. Is reporting being used or needed?
<--- Score

110. How accessible is the presenting problem as the treatment plan is designed?
<--- Score

111. Do the standards encompass all the changes that need to happen?
<--- Score

112. What quality tools were useful in the control phase?
<--- Score

113. Is there a documented and implemented monitoring plan?
<--- Score

Add up total points for this section:
_____ = Total points for this section

Divided by: ______ (number of

statements answered) = ______
Average score for this section

Transfer your score to the Assertive Community Treatment Index at the beginning of the Self-Assessment.

CRITERION #7: SUSTAIN:

INTENT: Retain the benefits.

In my belief, the answer to this question is clearly defined:

5 Strongly Agree

4 Agree

3 Neutral

2 Disagree

1 Strongly Disagree

1. Is compulsory community treatment ever justified?
<--- Score

2. Is your treatment culturally competent?
<--- Score

3. Are you familiar with a stage-wise approach to substance use treatment?
<--- Score

4. What are the best conditions for work based on mental effort?
<--- Score

5. How is assertive community treatment different from other services?
<--- Score

6. What records will be used/ provided for performance purposes?
<--- Score

7. Is all the evidence in?
<--- Score

8. Which types of treatment are provided to participants?
<--- Score

9. What is important to you in this area?
<--- Score

10. How do you help clients set goals?
<--- Score

11. Is it acceptable to stagger staff schedules to work later some evenings during the week and give them 9 to 5 hours during other days of the week?
<--- Score

12. Is your organization well-connected with a diverse group of community stakeholders?
<--- Score

13. How often do participants attend individual

treatment sessions during the last phase?
<--- Score

14. Why are community treatment orders controversial?
<--- Score

15. What kinds of training would interest you?
<--- Score

16. What is a human service professional?
<--- Score

17. What did the leader do before the exercise began?
<--- Score

18. What part of your job do you enjoy the most?
<--- Score

19. Can assertive community treatment remedy clients dropping out of treatment due to fragmented services?
<--- Score

20. What happens when that service leaves you injured, either physically or mentally?
<--- Score

21. How do you get them services?
<--- Score

22. Who is supposed to inform clients of switching practices?
<--- Score

23. Is gap recovery navigation (peer supports) a billable service by providers?
<--- Score

24. Do better mental models of AI lead to higher team performance?
<--- Score

25. Why is empathy considered an essential service mentality?
<--- Score

26. What resources will you call upon to help you maintain or restore your resilience?
<--- Score

27. How do you perform bottom-up services modification?
<--- Score

28. Have any staff members had training in the use of rewards and sanctions to modify the behavior of mental health participants?
<--- Score

29. Have you ever been placed on a community treatment order?
<--- Score

30. Are you currently undergoing treatment for a mental illness, condition or disorder?
<--- Score

31. User involvement in mental health nursing practice: rhetoric or reality?
<--- Score

32. Should psychiatric clients be granted access to organization records?
<--- Score

33. What are the mental tasks associated with good golf?
<--- Score

34. How many consumers are currently served by the team?
<--- Score

35. How do community treatment orders clarify practices of power?
<--- Score

36. What is an example from your own experiences of being on the same page with others on your team?
<--- Score

37. How does psychiatry relate to users of psychiatric services?
<--- Score

38. What organizations operate the program?
<--- Score

39. Is it an administrative activity?
<--- Score

40. What is your organization of the evidence?
<--- Score

41. Who is assertive community treatment for?

<--- Score

42. What is the length of treatment sessions?
<--- Score

43. Do you have sufficient staff resources assigned to the marketing function?
<--- Score

44. Does your team employ harm reduction tactics?
<--- Score

45. What do you expect once the referral is made?
<--- Score

46. Are there any mental health diagnoses that you do not accept in the mental health program?
<--- Score

47. Does the service user have a known physical condition that may inhibit cardiopulmonary function?
<--- Score

48. Do you have the same treatment targets as your psychiatric colleagues?
<--- Score

49. How are recovery and increased independence being addressed in your intervention/service?
<--- Score

50. How was your mental health program initially funded (start-up)?
<--- Score

51. Is a psychiatrist part of the team?
<--- Score

52. What is the quality of the evidence?
<--- Score

53. Is there consensus at your organization (and in your community) to implement ACT?
<--- Score

54. What services are available?
<--- Score

55. The customer experience lifecycle can stretch over decades and encompass thousands of interactions, all of which inform the mental state of individual customers. How do you keep track and manage this?
<--- Score

56. What works to promote workplace mental wellbeing?
<--- Score

57. Do you have significant experience at contract negotiation and management?
<--- Score

58. What are the goals and objectives of the project, service, or activity?
<--- Score

59. What is driving involuntary treatment in the community?
<--- Score

60. What is the difference between knowledge and quackery?
<--- Score

61. Are the intended settings for each service clear?
<--- Score

62. How do effective organizations go about creating a culture of shared goals rather than a culture of internal competition with a silo mentality?
<--- Score

63. How can certain mental models become instituted through policy as behavioural organizations?
<--- Score

64. How do you sup port your staff members in efforts?
<--- Score

65. How is the service currently organized to achieve successful transition?
<--- Score

66. Have you chosen a mental model to fit your preference?
<--- Score

67. What population does the program serve?
<--- Score

68. What is your mental model of negotiation?

<--- Score

69. What type of leadership style exists within your organization/practice or organization?
<--- Score

70. To what extent is your revenue diversified?
<--- Score

71. Why do so many people try so hard to avoid contacting psychiatric services?
<--- Score

72. Have you obtained and incorporated information from the referral source and/or team?
<--- Score

73. What application do you use?
<--- Score

74. What kinds of new services should be in place in five years time?
<--- Score

75. What is an Evidence-Based Practice?
<--- Score

76. How do ACT clients compare with the already stated receiving organization treatment?
<--- Score

77. How much tension is there among members in your team?
<--- Score

78. How do you ask for a second opinion?

<--- Score

79. Did the project come in on time, on budget, and of a quality staff can be proud of ?
<--- Score

80. How many clients are reviewed at each meeting?
<--- Score

81. What are the currently available resources (people, knowledge, community, money)?
<--- Score

82. How does the RTC administer and assess the effectiveness of psychiatric medications?
<--- Score

83. Do geriatric interventions reduce emergency department visits?
<--- Score

84. How does your team view abstinence versus reduction of use?
<--- Score

85. What are the policies when you do a home visit?
<--- Score

86. How can organizations realistically work towards a one business, one goal mentality?
<--- Score

87. Which aspects may be considered and with whom?

<--- Score

88. Will this position lead to a programmatic/ administrative simplification?
<--- Score

89. Is there a way for supply chain leaders, in particular, to step off the treadmill and escape a perpetual crisis mentality?
<--- Score

90. How many people are mentally checking out or may be part of a second wave of exits?
<--- Score

91. Have you ever been involuntarily committed to a state mental organization?
<--- Score

92. What have you heard about service?
<--- Score

93. Does the service publish any regular reports of activities/outcomes?
<--- Score

94. What changed your ability to be committed to and complete treatment?
<--- Score

95. Do you have a project or a program mentality?
<--- Score

96. What challenges have the program faced in operating?
<--- Score

97. Do you work directly with any stakeholders services departments?
<--- Score

98. What community departments will the client be utilizing?
<--- Score

99. Are there reasons why a request to change a primary care provider may be denied?
<--- Score

100. Are there any strategies to lower the mental burden of feeling watched?
<--- Score

101. What type of services are available?
<--- Score

102. Does your team suffer from poor shared mental models?
<--- Score

103. Do you have a strong desire to provide outstanding psychiatry services?
<--- Score

104. Are you aware of any physical medical condition that may contribute to the clients mental impairment?
<--- Score

105. Are the effects of cognitive remediation therapy (CRT) durable?
<--- Score

106. Is there evidence that cognitive behaviour therapy is an effective treatment?
<--- Score

107. What services are being provided?
<--- Score

108. Is treatment for substance abuse effective?
<--- Score

109. When things get slow, do you ask for more work?
<--- Score

110. Where in time (and mental space) is HR?
<--- Score

111. How do you find a psychiatrist?
<--- Score

112. Is there evidence that the individual has persistence?
<--- Score

113. What are the strengths of the CM ?
<--- Score

114. Is the information written in a basic reading level, available in languages of people served, and available in alternative formats?
<--- Score

115. What is assertive community treatment (ACT)?
<--- Score

116. What you do differently?
<--- Score

117. When do the services limits reset?
<--- Score

118. Can focus be used in individual treatment?
<--- Score

119. How does someone get screened for serious mental illness criteria?
<--- Score

120. Where do you send the referral?
<--- Score

121. What does the network look like for tele-psychiatry?
<--- Score

122. Do you say no to them and they accept it?
<--- Score

123. What is the role of the members of the team?
<--- Score

124. Are mental, physical and social aspects taken into account?
<--- Score

125. What partnerships are in place to help clients gain access to mental health services if some are not provided within the health service organization?
<--- Score

126. What unintended outcomes exist based on the current climate and culture?
<--- Score

127. Are community treatment orders really necessary for clients on ACT teams?
<--- Score

128. Do you have access to stakeholders services or funding for your participants?
<--- Score

129. What are the multiple criteria that indicate a employee may be mentally gifted?
<--- Score

130. What services do homeless people use?
<--- Score

131. What does success look like?
<--- Score

132. How good do you think you are at mental simulation?
<--- Score

133. How can the relation to the client be fostered and strengthened?
<--- Score

134. How many calls does the program receive?
<--- Score

135. What services can be provided via telephone?
<--- Score

136. Are the services provided in a manner that is beneficial or usable to the client?
<--- Score

137. What is assertive community treatment?
<--- Score

138. When is a psychiatric/psychological injury one which arises out of reasonable management action taken in a reasonable way?
<--- Score

139. Who is able to refer to your service?
<--- Score

140. Are there people who break the public laws, norms, or social conventions?
<--- Score

141. Have you ever sought treatment for your inability to handle stress?
<--- Score

142. What mental models in organizations?
<--- Score

143. How do you move from compliance to confidence to commitment in a team or organization?
<--- Score

144. How does this fit your users mental model?
<--- Score

145. What are the formal and informal roles and

activities of the already stated most influential actors?
<--- Score

146. What is the minimum age for someone to provide peer support services?
<--- Score

147. Should there be separate psychiatric services for ethnic minority groups?
<--- Score

148. What are your weak spots regarding the tasks?
<--- Score

149. Did you see a psychiatrist while in the service?
<--- Score

150. Do you provide direct services to clients?
<--- Score

151. Are there specific elements that should screen consumers into the treatment protocol?
<--- Score

152. Did you receive any medical or mental-health treatment?
<--- Score

153. How often does your mental health program have regular meetings (staffings) where participant progress is considered?
<--- Score

154. Would you be able to describe your mental

model to others?
<--- Score

155. Can acs accept pa requests for old / ending services on the new request form?
<--- Score

156. Can effectiveness, efficiency, and performance transparency be ensured?
<--- Score

157. What information would you like to have?
<--- Score

158. Which, if any, methods, does the team use?
<--- Score

159. What form will supervision records take?
<--- Score

160. Are there specific counseling approaches more congruent with the beliefs of most members?
<--- Score

161. What length of time is the contract term?
<--- Score

162. What are the gaps that currently exist for diagnosis and treatment in the community?
<--- Score

163. Who can benefit from ACT services?
<--- Score

164. Have you received any medical or mental

health treatment?
<--- Score

165. What, if any, other funding sources has your mental health program obtained throughout its history?
<--- Score

166. Is the work / job what you expected?
<--- Score

167. How will you know the crisis has passed?
<--- Score

168. Is there a written policy and procedure manual for your mental health program?
<--- Score

169. Are there any limits to any covered services?
<--- Score

170. How does it fit into the system of care?
<--- Score

171. Does the probation service provide any special support for the mentally ill?
<--- Score

172. What do you know about accountability and outcomes?
<--- Score

173. What does the treatment consist of?
<--- Score

174. How do you choose an OB/GYN?

<--- Score

175. How is assertive Business Value Reporting treatment different from other services?
<--- Score

176. Is customer services the final answer?
<--- Score

177. How do you find out more about assertive community treatment?
<--- Score

178. Is/are the mental health (and substance abuse, if applicable) treatment provider(s) directly contracted with the program?
<--- Score

179. Do community organizations provide a viable pathway to a baccalaureate degree?
<--- Score

180. Who gets a Community Treatment Order?
<--- Score

181. What should you do on a follow-up visit?
<--- Score

182. Does anyone else also undertake caring responsibilities for the person?
<--- Score

183. What substance abuse resources are available in the community?
<--- Score

184. What barriers have you had to getting services?
<--- Score

185. What types of ocs are associated with schizophrenia?
<--- Score

186. Has your nonprofit ever applied to the Community Foundation?
<--- Score

187. Do you encourage participation in community based peer support?
<--- Score

188. With the addition of new ACT teams, is there any consideration for flexibility for the prescriber positions?
<--- Score

189. How many topics are recommended for treatment?
<--- Score

190. Are mobile phones and handheld computers being used to enhance delivery of psychiatric treatment?
<--- Score

191. What organizations operate programs?
<--- Score

192. How is the Crisis Line staffed during the week and on the weekends?
<--- Score

193. What are your ethical obligations to existing clients?
<--- Score

194. Is jail used as one of the possible sanctions in your mental health program?
<--- Score

195. What are the reasons clients have been turned away?
<--- Score

196. Does your state provide services under comprehensive community-based mental health service systems?
<--- Score

197. How do you make a referral?
<--- Score

198. Does stress lead to a loss of team perspective?
<--- Score

199. Is person interested in PACT services?
<--- Score

200. Is there evidence of dependence?
<--- Score

201. How is your mental health program currently funded?
<--- Score

202. Do mentally ill offenders have access to treatment?

<--- Score

203. Can people who have had long stays in psychiatric organizations be supported to live independently in the community?
<--- Score

204. Is there evidence that cognitive behaviour therapy is an effective treatment for schizophrenia?
<--- Score

205. What is the suggested format for organization Supervisor-Based Training?
<--- Score

206. How did you get to the emergency department?
<--- Score

207. How does mental toughness (and resilience) influence career success outcomes?
<--- Score

208. How do you file for mental disability?
<--- Score

209. What new services will be provided and what are the skills involved?
<--- Score

210. What are the new sources of power that emerge in recovery-oriented care?
<--- Score

211. Is the program showing signs of a fortress

mentality ?
<--- Score

212. Are day organizations necessary?
<--- Score

213. Where do you find the care coordination forms?
<--- Score

214. How is it possible to change the collective Mindset from a Silo Mentality to a Challenge Intelligence in your own organizations?
<--- Score

215. What is your target group you aim to work with?
<--- Score

216. Do existing policies and procedures at your organization support model implementation?
<--- Score

217. Effective community treatment of the chronically mentally ill: What is necessary?
<--- Score

218. How large companies can stand out and succeed employing a start-up mentality and culture internally?
<--- Score

219. What are your organizations ACT admission and discharge criteria?
<--- Score

220. Are treatment and community support resources available for as much time as necessary?
<--- Score

221. Is it possible to relax the restriction on the definition of collaterals to include paid providers and other individuals in the community?
<--- Score

222. What are the minimum and maximum clients allowed per group?
<--- Score

223. How much of your time is allocated specifically to the ACT team?
<--- Score

224. What service component is being provided to the client?
<--- Score

225. Does your mental health program have regular meetings where participant progress is considered (e.g., staffing or pre-program meetings)?
<--- Score

226. What type of technical assistance is available to your organization to help get started?
<--- Score

227. Where do you get your clients from?
<--- Score

228. What is considered to be an out of state community based residential placement and what

is considered to be an out of state non-community based residential placement?
<--- Score

229. Which is the primary service function of rehabilitation services?
<--- Score

230. To what extent does your MIS integrate information from various programs and sites?
<--- Score

231. Are the cybersecurity fundamentals you started with so many years ago still sound today?
<--- Score

232. What are the main gaps in the community treatment system?
<--- Score

233. Is there evidence of intoxication?
<--- Score

234. Is child care offered for participants with small children when the participants are engaged in mental health program activities?
<--- Score

235. What primary mental health diagnoses do your current participants have?
<--- Score

236. What are the policy observations for the Assertive Community Treatment program?
<--- Score

237. What evidence is there that a multi-professional approach to staffing is being deployed across your organization?
<--- Score

238. How do mental models affect design?
<--- Score

239. How do you know when you reach a goal?
<--- Score

240. Did you know the roles and responsibilities of others on your team?
<--- Score

241. Does one organization provide treatment to the majority of the participants?
<--- Score

242. What are you doing with regard to employment or education?
<--- Score

243. How do you build up and foster networks?
<--- Score

244. What values and principles seem most important to leadership based on actions and practices?
<--- Score

245. What does the revolutionary nature of transformation involve?
<--- Score

246. What are the activities and roles of the most

important actors?
<--- Score

247. How efficient has the use of the methods and resources been?
<--- Score

248. Do you have an advisory committee/board?
<--- Score

249. What are evidence-based practices?
<--- Score

250. Does your organization conduct mental health and personality testing?
<--- Score

251. What has changed in you, either or both physically and mentally since participating in the program?
<--- Score

252. What mental blockchain from the program stands out in your mind?
<--- Score

253. When does one have the right to ask for an appeal?
<--- Score

254. Integrating mental health and chemical dependency treatment: What does the research tell you?
<--- Score

255. Is the mental model too complex?

<--- Score

256. Who are the key organizational stakeholders to advise and assist with community response to a critical incident involving a employee-athlete?
<--- Score

257. Which member of the team or support system will provide the service?
<--- Score

258. What services have you been using?
<--- Score

259. How will supervision records be used?
<--- Score

260. What community support services can be utilised (alone or to supplement other interventions)?
<--- Score

261. Cbt for ptsd in severe mental illness: what are the additive benefits of cognitive restructuring to education and breathing retraining?
<--- Score

262. What things influence keeping clients stuck?
<--- Score

263. What does your manager do to support you to stay mentally healthy at work?
<--- Score

264. What are the obstacles to user/carer involvement in organizational change?

<--- Score

265. What are the functions of the record?
<--- Score

266. What kinds of services do you provide?
<--- Score

267. What works for people with mental retardation?
<--- Score

268. Is silo mentality hurting your customer experience?
<--- Score

269. What is the Program of Assertive Community Treatment?
<--- Score

270. Should you add outpatient services or otherwise diversify?
<--- Score

271. What are your ethical obligations to new clients who are transgender with respect to diagnosing them in record?
<--- Score

272. What is the follow on for failure to appear for treatment?
<--- Score

273. How do you strengthen a community?
<--- Score

274. Housing homeless people with severe mental illness: why safe havens?
<--- Score

275. What is the difference between a provider and a service provider?
<--- Score

276. What would you like to have happen in the future?
<--- Score

277. Where do you see people from the ACT team the most?
<--- Score

278. Is it acceptable to allow research in a community that cannot afford the treatment being tested?
<--- Score

279. Who can be contacted if your main support person cannot be contacted in a crisis?
<--- Score

280. Have you ever been declared incompetent by reason of mental defect or disease by any court of competent jurisdiction?
<--- Score

281. Does treatment delay in first-episode psychosis really matter?
<--- Score

282. Is the recommended intensity for each service consistent with the intended role of that service?

<--- Score

283. Do you have any psychiatric or psychological treatment history?
<--- Score

284. What might prompt removing an individual (termination) from participation in the mental health program?
<--- Score

285. Are there social or community supports?
<--- Score

286. How many staff work on the ACT team?
<--- Score

287. How often do participants attend group treatment sessions during the last phase?
<--- Score

288. What is the employees current mental status?
<--- Score

289. What is your favorite part about being on an ACT team?
<--- Score

290. Is there a reproducibility crisis?
<--- Score

291. Does your current caring arrangements continue over time without more services or support?
<--- Score

292. How many psychiatric clients in prison?
<--- Score

293. Does it take additional unnecessary mental effort?
<--- Score

294. Which of your clients is it inappropriate to write a letter for?
<--- Score

295. Where do you see yourself a year from now?
<--- Score

296. Do you know your colleagues mental models?
<--- Score

297. Are emergency dental services covered?
<--- Score

298. Is there a difference in transportation of psychiatric clients to the emergency department?
<--- Score

299. What are the strategies that you use when you assist with skill practice?
<--- Score

300. What are service users and carers telling you about the quality of services you provide?
<--- Score

301. What would have helped to keep your child at home and in the community?
<--- Score

302. How many treatment provider departments work directly with your mental health program?
<--- Score

303. Can the treatment of substance misuse and mental health be integrated?
<--- Score

304. How do you establish competence?
<--- Score

305. What are the classes of mental illness?
<--- Score

306. What evidence is there that clients with long-term conditions would welcome a shift to primary and community-based treatment for own conditions?
<--- Score

307. What mental steps do you go through before taking some action?
<--- Score

308. Is it based on /informed by evidence?
<--- Score

309. What service gaps do you perceive?
<--- Score

310. What is the Community that the project is intended to serve?
<--- Score

311. Where are the most glaring gaps in a communitys continuum of treatment, social

services, and supports?
<--- Score

312. How are consumers involved as members of your team?
<--- Score

313. Is your treatment strengths-based?
<--- Score

314. When does the onset of many serious mental illnesses begin?
<--- Score

315. Are providers aware of what services are being billed under name?
<--- Score

316. Why cross-disciplinary theories of team cognition?
<--- Score

317. Is the person able and willing to engage with treatment and support options?
<--- Score

318. Is there evidence of impulsivity in past?
<--- Score

319. Does your organization/practice use evidence-based or evidence-supported protocols?
<--- Score

320. With corresponding changes in the mental demands on future leaders, how will you produce corresponding capacities of thinking?

<--- Score

321. Do specialized service providers exist that operate best-of-breed technologies to support the environmental and economic objectives of a reverse logistics system?
<--- Score

322. Is client considered and accepted into the ACT treatment program?
<--- Score

323. Does your program place clients in jobs that are permanent?
<--- Score

324. What variables mediate and moderate program effects?
<--- Score

325. Who does the Assertive Community Treatment program serve?
<--- Score

326. Are there spiritual organizations/groups you would like to belong to?
<--- Score

327. What specific evidence-based practices does your organization currently use?
<--- Score

328. Who in your local mental health system would benefit from ACTs intensive level of care?
<--- Score

329. What models are operating in other states?
<--- Score

330. Do staff at your organization provide benefits counseling for people on SSI/SSDI?
<--- Score

331. When do you stop calling the Program Specialists for technical assistance?
<--- Score

332. How effective is targeted advertising?
<--- Score

333. Must the participant be amenable to mental health treatment to be eligible for the program?
<--- Score

334. How well do the team members communicate about the home visit?
<--- Score

335. Do shared goals really enhance team innovation?
<--- Score

336. Measuring consumer participation in mental health services: are attitudes related to professional orientation?
<--- Score

337. How much friction is there among members in your team?
<--- Score

338. What billable services may be used to assist a

recipient with supported employment?
<--- Score

339. What is the average length of treatment?
<--- Score

340. Do social welfare services provide the mentally ill with any special support after release?
<--- Score

341. Does the mental model match the application physical workflow?
<--- Score

342. How effectively does the individual perform the skill when it is first modeled?
<--- Score

343. What is mental health consultation?
<--- Score

344. What do you know about providing services to people who are homeless?
<--- Score

345. Which parts of the program were most useful to you?
<--- Score

346. How are services approved and authorized?
<--- Score

347. How do you design an action program for change?
<--- Score

348. How might it do harm to physical or mental integrity?
<--- Score

349. What type of facilities support service users?
<--- Score

350. What constitutes evidence of oppression?
<--- Score

351. How will you find out if services are denied?
<--- Score

352. Are past treatment efforts asked about and understood?
<--- Score

353. What treatment is provided for the mentally ill?
<--- Score

354. What do you know about the current service?
<--- Score

355. Do you have a window or a back out period when participants can try the mental health program and decide not to participate?
<--- Score

356. How many clients are you currently working with?
<--- Score

357. How will your program support a childs transition from residential care back to the community?

<--- Score

358. What mental health resources and opioid treatment centers are available in your communities?
<--- Score

359. Has your organization/practice trained staff to use the protocols with clients?
<--- Score

360. Does applicant have current or history of substance abuse?
<--- Score

361. Does the assertive outreach team regularly collaborate with culturally specific community organizations?
<--- Score

362. What factors facilitate user/carer involvement in organizational change?
<--- Score

363. What recruitment procedures do you use to find clients for the ACT team?
<--- Score

364. Which would be considered a psychiatric rehabilitation service approach?
<--- Score

365. What is it that is stopping user knowledge from being acknowledged?
<--- Score

366. Who makes referrals to the ACT team?
<--- Score

367. What do you feel are your greatest strengths?
<--- Score

368. How are intra-organizational silos and silo mentality generated?
<--- Score

369. Do you know what you cannot do, and what do you do?
<--- Score

370. How well do your organizations existing services and structures match up (or not) with ACT core components and critical ingredients?
<--- Score

371. How do you assure that there is no conflict of interest from provider to the consumer?
<--- Score

372. What is attitude to help seeking/treatment?
<--- Score

373. What barriers have the target population faced in accessing the program?
<--- Score

374. Does organization have resources to provide services?
<--- Score

375. Where do calls to the Crisis Line come from?
<--- Score

376. Is the treatment (protocol implementation) staff following the protocol?
<--- Score

377. How does an individual become a client of the ACT team?
<--- Score

378. How often do you see the team psychiatrist?
<--- Score

379. Does the current service-delivery culture in your organization support the ACT model?
<--- Score

380. What is the length of treatment?
<--- Score

381. What would you like from the service?
<--- Score

382. How has crisis situations been dealt with in the past?
<--- Score

383. What is the average length of time of a typical meeting?
<--- Score

384. Is it possible for you or any other psychiatrist who has knowledge to bring an ethics complaint?
<--- Score

385. How do you go about establishing credibility?
<--- Score

386. What skill(s) do you want them to have?
<--- Score

387. When was your mental health program program implemented?
<--- Score

388. Evidence-based behavioral rehabilitation in persons with severe mental illness: who benefits and why?
<--- Score

389. What are your strengths regarding the tasks?
<--- Score

390. Who benefits from jail diversion?
<--- Score

391. How often are there conflicts about ideas in your team?
<--- Score

392. Do you empower clients by providing them with information on rights?
<--- Score

393. Do shared mental models stifle or promote team creativity?
<--- Score

394. How often are there disagreements about resource allocation in your team?
<--- Score

395. Has treatment for your mental health

program participants been funded from different sources? Which?
<--- Score

396. Are you a specialist in any areas?
<--- Score

397. Is it enough that the mental models be shared, or should the models themselves also be consistent with evidence-based knowledge?
<--- Score

398. What are the obstacles and barriers to providing continuity of care for people with SMI?
<--- Score

399. Is there physical or mental difficulty in executing the actions?
<--- Score

400. Will it be a conflict of interest if you refer your clients there?
<--- Score

401. How do you file a complaint?
<--- Score

402. Has it been hard to bring an environmental message to your clients?
<--- Score

403. What works for whom in a computer-mediated communication intervention in community psychiatry?
<--- Score

404. How does the Assertive Community Treatment program work?
<--- Score

405. Does the individual have the mental, physical, and emotional capacity to perform?
<--- Score

406. What are the arguments and the evidence in the field?
<--- Score

407. Is assertive community treatment effective?
<--- Score

408. What services are not covered?
<--- Score

409. How was community input collected?
<--- Score

410. Is the new program eligible to be licensed before all team members complete training?
<--- Score

411. What characteristics of ACT programs help to facilitate communication among team members?
<--- Score

412. What methods does the team use to keep clients involved in ACT?
<--- Score

413. What is the total number of staff positions on the ACT team?
<--- Score

414. How often does the ACT team meet as a full group to review services provided to each client?
<--- Score

415. Is seeking safety considered a crisis intervention?
<--- Score

416. What services have been involved in the past?
<--- Score

417. Has a replacement memo outlining billable services been put up?
<--- Score

418. How do you work towards shared goals?
<--- Score

419. Why do some organizations adopt environmental management practices that go beyond regulatory compliance?
<--- Score

420. How many of your clients have a psychiatric disability?
<--- Score

421. When assessing unknown contamination of an environmental sample, where does the chemist begin?
<--- Score

422. How much are personality conflicts evident in your team?
<--- Score

423. Does the individual show the mental flexibility to quickly evolve thinking based on others inputs?
<--- Score

424. What was missing from the program for you?
<--- Score

425. What works for people with mental retardation ?
<--- Score

426. Are there any other key tasks, which would be essential to initial implementation?
<--- Score

427. Is there evidence of an acute change in mental status from the residents baseline?
<--- Score

428. Do you want to make changes to the mental health delivery system in the community?
<--- Score

429. Are admission, treatment, and discharge criteria in place and used consistently by staff?
<--- Score

430. What strategies should a treatment provider consider?
<--- Score

431. Do you have a specific target population?
<--- Score

432. What do you know about addressing homelessness?
<--- Score

433. How to ensure potential barriers are resolved for the target population to access the program?
<--- Score

434. Is the person currently engaged in any treatment?
<--- Score

435. How has theoretical research in psychiatric Epigenetics fared in the light of experimental evidence?
<--- Score

436. Can emergency psychiatry be person-centred?
<--- Score

437. What do you think are your greatest strengths?
<--- Score

438. What are community treatment services?
<--- Score

439. What kind of vocational services have you received in the past?
<--- Score

440. Which of the tasks subject you to the most mental workload?
<--- Score

441. Why is it important to spend time confronting faulty mental models?
<--- Score

442. Which are core principles of psychiatric rehabilitation?
<--- Score

443. How long do you stay in the program?
<--- Score

444. Are individuals with specific conditions shunned from the community?
<--- Score

445. What is the nature of the calls received by the Crisis Line?
<--- Score

446. What else would you want to see as part of the training?
<--- Score

447. How do you maintain good physical and mental health?
<--- Score

448. What are key milestones for building a true service-centric mentality?
<--- Score

449. What are the best practices for treatment?
<--- Score

450. Will the customer suffer mentally or physically by delaying or not purchasing?

<--- Score

451. Is this in the best interests of your client?
<--- Score

452. How do you ask for an expedited appeal?
<--- Score

453. What is the Assertive Community Treatment program?
<--- Score

454. How important is your leisure time and your physical and mental wellbeing to you?
<--- Score

455. What are you going to do next session?
<--- Score

456. What is the difference between an evidence-based practice protocol and a best practice protocol?
<--- Score

457. What does the mental health team and organization DEM expect of the paramedics?
<--- Score

458. What formal admission criteria do you use to screen potential clients?
<--- Score

459. Do you perform drug testing to ensure mental health participants are using prescribed mental health medications appropriately?
<--- Score

460. Does the fee-earner have a mental block on the file?
<--- Score

461. What do readers mental models tell you about transgender persons?
<--- Score

462. How does the value emerge in customers practices (also from mental and emotional experiences)?
<--- Score

463. Can the client concentrate on a simple mental task, as counting backwards or adding numbers?
<--- Score

464. How often are there differences of opinion in your team?
<--- Score

465. In what ways do you obtain status or be seen as a success?
<--- Score

466. What should you do if you have a complaint?
<--- Score

467. When does the principle of implied consent apply to mentally incompetent adults?
<--- Score

468. What mental accounts do you have in your mind about purchasing products or services?
<--- Score

469. Have essential records been reviewed?
<--- Score

470. Is this rtc providing 24-hour inpatient care with observation and supervision by mental health professionals?
<--- Score

471. How do you treat schizophrenia in persons with ID?
<--- Score

472. Are there circumstances where you have to take clients onto your team?
<--- Score

473. What mental image from the program stands out in your mind?
<--- Score

474. How should it be funded?
<--- Score

475. How sure are you of the assessment?
<--- Score

476. What are the strengths of the client?
<--- Score

477. Are the views of mental health user groups representative of the already stated of ordinary clients?
<--- Score

478. Are you currently enrolled in organization or

any other educational program?
<--- Score

479. Should service user involvement be consigned to history?
<--- Score

480. Street outreach for homeless persons with serious mental illness: is it effective?
<--- Score

481. Do actions lead to a shift in mindset and mental models within the broader environment?
<--- Score

482. Is a comprehensive review of records labor intensive?
<--- Score

483. How much emotional conflict is there among members in your team?
<--- Score

484. Does involuntary outpatient commitment lead to more intensive treatment?
<--- Score

485. How do you change a organizations whole business mentality?
<--- Score

486. What is one change is your team facing presently?
<--- Score

487. Do you have to have a referral?

<--- Score

488. What challenges or barriers exist in trying to provide this service in a rural setting?
<--- Score

489. Are there personal characteristics that make cognitive change more or less likely?
<--- Score

490. Does involuntary outpatient treatment work?
<--- Score

491. How does path interface with your stakeholders service continuum?
<--- Score

492. What is the projected demand for treatment in the community?
<--- Score

Add up total points for this section:
_____ = Total points for this section

Divided by: ______ (number of statements answered) = ______ Average score for this section

Transfer your score to the Assertive Community Treatment Index at the beginning of the Self-Assessment.

Assertive Community Treatment and Managing Projects, Criteria for Project Managers:

1.0 Initiating Process Group: Assertive Community Treatment

1. Which six sigma dmaic phase focuses on why and how defects and errors occur?

2. Who is involved in each phase?

3. The Assertive Community Treatment project you are managing has nine stakeholders. How many channel of communications are there between corresponding stakeholders?

4. Were resources available as planned?

5. During which stage of Risk planning are risks prioritized based on probability and impact?

6. For technology Assertive Community Treatment projects only: Are all production support stakeholders (Business unit, technical support, & user) prepared for implementation with appropriate contingency plans?

7. What will be the pressing issues of tomorrow?

8. How can you make your needs known?

9. What areas does the group agree are the biggest success on the Assertive Community Treatment project?

10. In which Assertive Community Treatment project management process group is the detailed Assertive Community Treatment project budget created?

11. Do you understand the quality and control criteria that must be achieved for successful Assertive Community Treatment project completion?

12. Are you properly tracking the progress of the Assertive Community Treatment project and communicating the status to stakeholders?

13. What are the pressing issues of the hour?

14. Who does what?

15. Just how important is your work to the overall success of the Assertive Community Treatment project?

16. What were the challenges that you encountered during the execution of a previous Assertive Community Treatment project that you would not want to repeat?

17. How is each deliverable reviewed, verified, and validated?

18. Professionals want to know what is expected from them what are the deliverables?

19. Have the stakeholders identified all individual requirements pertaining to business process?

20. What will you do?

1.1 Project Charter: Assertive Community Treatment

21. Pop quiz – which are the same inputs as in the Assertive Community Treatment project charter?

22. Are there special technology requirements?

23. Whose input and support will this Assertive Community Treatment project require?

24. When do you use a Assertive Community Treatment project Charter?

25. Strategic fit: what is the strategic initiative identifier for this Assertive Community Treatment project?

26. Will this replace an existing product?

27. Must Have?

28. Why executive support?

29. Who is the sponsor?

30. Where does all this information come from?

31. What metrics could you look at?

32. Fit with other Products Compliments – Cannibalizes?

33. What are you striving to accomplish (measurable goal(s))?

34. What are you trying to accomplish?

35. Who are the stakeholders?

36. Is time of the essence?

37. What are some examples of a business case?

38. What are the deliverables?

39. What does it need to do?

40. When will this occur?

1.2 Stakeholder Register: Assertive Community Treatment

41. Who wants to talk about Security?

42. How much influence do they have on the Assertive Community Treatment project?

43. What & Why?

44. Who is managing stakeholder engagement?

45. What is the power of the stakeholder?

46. What opportunities exist to provide communications?

47. Is your organization ready for change?

48. How big is the gap?

49. What are the major Assertive Community Treatment project milestones requiring communications or providing communications opportunities?

50. How will reports be created?

51. How should employers make voices heard?

1.3 Stakeholder Analysis Matrix: Assertive Community Treatment

52. Seasonality, weather effects?

53. Are there two or three that rise to the top, and a couple that are sliding to the bottom?

54. Supporters; who are the supporters?

55. Disadvantages of proposition?

56. Are there different rules or organizational models for men and women?

57. Why do you need to manage Assertive Community Treatment project Risk?

58. Advantages of proposition?

59. Who is most dependent on the resources at stake?

60. What mechanisms are proposed to monitor and measure Assertive Community Treatment project performance in terms of social development outcomes?

61. Does your organization have bad debt or cash-flow problems?

62. Who is influential in the Assertive Community Treatment project area (both thematic and geographic areas)?

63. Who has not been involved up to now and should have been?

64. How will the Assertive Community Treatment project benefit them?

65. Who has been involved in the area (thematic or geographic) in the past?

66. Volumes, production, economies?

67. What do you Evaluate?

68. What can the stakeholder prevent from happening?

69. New USPs?

70. Which conditions out of the control of the management are crucial for the achievement of the outputs?

71. Geographical, export, import?

2.0 Planning Process Group: Assertive Community Treatment

72. You did your readings, yes?

73. What business situation is being addressed?

74. How will you do it?

75. Mitigate. what will you do to minimize the impact should a risk event occur?

76. Just how important is your work to the overall success of the Assertive Community Treatment project?

77. Do the partners have sufficient financial capacity to keep up the benefits produced by the programme?

78. How are it Assertive Community Treatment projects different?

79. When developing the estimates for Assertive Community Treatment project phases, you choose to add the individual estimates for the activities that comprise each phase. What type of estimation method are you using?

80. Does it make any difference if you are successful?

81. In what ways can the governance of the Assertive Community Treatment project be improved so that it has greater likelihood of achieving future

sustainability?

82. If task x starts two days late, what is the effect on the Assertive Community Treatment project end date?

83. Are there efficient coordination mechanisms to avoid overloading the counterparts, participating stakeholders?

84. How do you integrate Assertive Community Treatment project Planning with the Iterative/ Evolutionary SDLC?

85. What are the different approaches to building the WBS?

86. First of all, should any action be taken?

87. Is your organization showing technical capacity and leadership commitment to keep working with the Assertive Community Treatment project and to repeat it?

88. To what extent and in what ways are the Assertive Community Treatment project contributing to progress towards organizational reform?

89. What type of estimation method are you using?

90. Are the follow-up indicators relevant and do they meet the quality needed to measure the outputs and outcomes of the Assertive Community Treatment project?

91. Who are the Assertive Community Treatment project stakeholders?

2.1 Project Management Plan: Assertive Community Treatment

92. Is mitigation authorized or recommended?

93. Are the existing and future without-plan conditions reasonable and appropriate?

94. Is the budget realistic?

95. What would you do differently?

96. What are the training needs?

97. What is Assertive Community Treatment project scope management?

98. Is the appropriate plan selected based on your organizations objectives and evaluation criteria expressed in Principles and Guidelines policies?

99. Do the proposed changes from the Assertive Community Treatment project include any significant risks to safety?

100. Who manages integration?

101. How well are you able to manage your risk?

102. Was the peer (technical) review of the cost estimates duly coordinated with the cost estimate center of expertise and addressed in the review documentation and certification?

103. Why do you manage integration?

104. Is the engineering content at a feasibility level-of-detail, and is it sufficiently complete, to provide an adequate basis for the baseline cost estimate?

105. What went right?

106. Did the planning effort collaborate to develop solutions that integrate expertise, policies, programs, and Assertive Community Treatment projects across entities?

107. What if, for example, the positive direction and vision of your organization causes expected trends to change resulting in greater need than expected?

108. Are there any client staffing expectations?

109. How can you best help your organization to develop consistent practices in Assertive Community Treatment project management planning stages?

2.2 Scope Management Plan: Assertive Community Treatment

110. Are stakeholders aware and supportive of the principles and practices of modern software estimation?

111. Is a pmo (Assertive Community Treatment project management office) in place and provide oversight to the Assertive Community Treatment project?

112. Are the schedule estimates reasonable given the Assertive Community Treatment project?

113. Is there an approved case?

114. What are the risks that could significantly affect the budget of the Assertive Community Treatment project?

115. Who is responsible for monitoring the Assertive Community Treatment project scope to ensure the Assertive Community Treatment project remains within the scope baseline?

116. Is each item clearly and completely defined?

117. Function of the configuration control board?

118. Are issues raised, assessed, actioned, and resolved in a timely and efficient manner?

119. Has your organization done similar tasks before?

120. Personnel with expertise?

121. Can each item be appropriately scheduled?

122. Is the assigned Assertive Community Treatment project manager a PMP (Certified Assertive Community Treatment project manager) and experienced?

123. Do you have the reasons why the changes to your organizational systems and capabilities are required?

124. Is current scope of the Assertive Community Treatment project substantially different than that originally defined?

125. Will the Assertive Community Treatment project deliverables become accepted in writing?

126. Time estimation – how much time will be needed?

127. Does the Assertive Community Treatment project team have the skills necessary to successfully complete current Assertive Community Treatment project(s) and support the application?

128. Are target dates established for each milestone deliverable?

129. Is the Assertive Community Treatment project status reviewed with the steering and executive teams at appropriate intervals?

2.3 Requirements Management Plan: Assertive Community Treatment

130. What is the earliest finish date for this Assertive Community Treatment project if it is scheduled to start on ...?

131. How will the information be distributed?

132. Could inaccurate or incomplete requirements in this Assertive Community Treatment project create a serious risk for the business?

133. Did you provide clear and concise specifications?

134. Will the contractors involved take full responsibility?

135. Are actual resource expenditures versus planned still acceptable?

136. Will the Assertive Community Treatment project requirements become approved in writing?

137. Will you perform a Requirements Risk assessment and develop a plan to deal with risks?

138. Who is responsible for quantifying the Assertive Community Treatment project requirements?

139. What information regarding the Assertive Community Treatment project requirements will be reported?

140. How will bidders price evaluations be done, by deliverables, phases, or in a big bang?

141. Are actual resources expenditures versus planned expenditures acceptable?

142. Subject to change control?

143. Is it new or replacing an existing business system or process?

144. Did you use declarative statements?

145. How will you communicate scheduled tasks to other team members?

146. What are you counting on?

147. Who came up with this requirement?

148. How will requirements be managed?

149. Is the system software (non-operating system) new to the IT Assertive Community Treatment project team?

2.4 Requirements Documentation: Assertive Community Treatment

150. What is the risk associated with the technology?

151. How does what is being described meet the business need?

152. What facilities must be supported by the system?

153. How will requirements be documented and who signs off on them?

154. What if the system wasn t implemented?

155. Where do system and software requirements come from, what are sources?

156. How do you know when a Requirement is accurate enough?

157. If applicable; are there issues linked with the fact that this is an offshore Assertive Community Treatment project?

158. Who is interacting with the system?

159. What can tools do for us?

160. What are current process problems?

161. Is your business case still valid?

162. Are there any requirements conflicts?

163. What is a show stopper in the requirements?

164. What are the potential disadvantages/ advantages?

165. Is the requirement properly understood?

166. How will they be documented / shared?

167. Do your constraints stand?

168. What variations exist for a process?

169. The problem with gathering requirements is right there in the word gathering. What images does it conjure?

2.5 Requirements Traceability Matrix: Assertive Community Treatment

170. How small is small enough?

171. Do you have a clear understanding of all subcontracts in place?

172. Why do you manage scope?

173. How will it affect the stakeholders personally in career?

174. Why use a WBS?

175. Describe the process for approving requirements so they can be added to the traceability matrix and Assertive Community Treatment project work can be performed. Will the Assertive Community Treatment project requirements become approved in writing?

176. What are the chronologies, contingencies, consequences, criteria?

177. How do you manage scope?

178. Is there a requirements traceability process in place?

179. Will you use a Requirements Traceability Matrix?

180. What percentage of Assertive Community Treatment projects are producing traceability

matrices between requirements and other work products?

181. What is the WBS?

2.6 Project Scope Statement: Assertive Community Treatment

182. Were potential customers involved early in the planning process?

183. Is the plan for your organization of the Assertive Community Treatment project resources adequate?

184. Is the plan for Assertive Community Treatment project resources adequate?

185. Is the Assertive Community Treatment project sponsor function identified and defined?

186. If the scope changes, what will the impact be to your Assertive Community Treatment project in terms of duration, cost, quality, or any other important areas of the Assertive Community Treatment project?

187. What are the major deliverables of the Assertive Community Treatment project?

188. Elements of scope management that deal with concept development ?

189. What is the product of this Assertive Community Treatment project?

190. Elements that deal with providing the detail?

191. Does the scope statement still need some clarity?

192. Will there be a Change Control Process in place?

193. Will the qa related information be reported regularly as part of the status reporting mechanisms?

194. If there are vendors, have they signed off on the Assertive Community Treatment project Plan?

195. How often do you estimate that the scope might change, and why?

196. Is there a Quality Assurance Plan documented and filed?

197. Will all tasks resulting from issues be entered into the Assertive Community Treatment project Plan and tracked through the plan?

198. Will the risk plan be updated on a regular and frequent basis?

199. Which risks does the Assertive Community Treatment project focus on?

200. Is the Assertive Community Treatment project organization documented and on file?

201. Will an issue form be in use?

2.7 Assumption and Constraint Log: Assertive Community Treatment

202. Do documented requirements exist for all critical components and areas, including technical, business, interfaces, performance, security and conversion requirements?

203. Are there processes in place to ensure that all the terms and code concepts have been documented consistently?

204. Can you perform this task or activity in a more effective manner?

205. Security analysis has access to information that is sanitized?

206. Are processes for release management of new development from coding and unit testing, to integration testing, to training, and production defined and followed?

207. What would you gain if you spent time working to improve this process?

208. Are you meeting your customers expectations consistently?

209. Is there documentation of system capability requirements, data requirements, environment requirements, security requirements, and computer and hardware requirements?

210. Do you know what your customers expectations are regarding this process?

211. When can log be discarded?

212. Is the amount of effort justified by the anticipated value of forming a new process?

213. What do you log?

214. Was the document/deliverable developed per the appropriate or required standards (for example, Institute of Electrical and Electronics Engineers standards)?

215. What if failure during recovery?

216. Is the process working, and people are not executing in compliance of the process?

217. Have the scope, objectives, costs, benefits and impacts been communicated to all involved and/or impacted stakeholders and work groups?

218. Does the traceability documentation describe the tool and/or mechanism to be used to capture traceability throughout the life cycle?

219. How can constraints be violated?

220. Are requirements management tracking tools and procedures in place?

221. Have you eliminated all duplicative tasks or manual efforts, where appropriate?

2.8 Work Breakdown Structure: Assertive Community Treatment

222. Is it still viable?

223. Can you make it?

224. How much detail?

225. Is it a change in scope?

226. How far down?

227. What is the probability that the Assertive Community Treatment project duration will exceed xx weeks?

228. What has to be done?

229. When does it have to be done?

230. Why would you develop a Work Breakdown Structure?

231. How big is a work-package?

232. Who has to do it?

233. When do you stop?

234. How many levels?

235. Where does it take place?

236. When would you develop a Work Breakdown Structure?

237. What is the probability of completing the Assertive Community Treatment project in less that xx days?

2.9 WBS Dictionary: Assertive Community Treatment

238. Does the scheduling system identify in a timely manner the status of work?

239. The Assertive Community Treatment projected business base for each period?

240. Are the variances between budgeted and actual indirect costs identified and analyzed at the level of assigned responsibility for control (indirect pool, department, etc.)?

241. Changes in the direct base to which overhead costs are allocated?

242. Are indirect costs accumulated for comparison with the corresponding budgets?

243. Do the lines of authority for incurring indirect costs correspond to the lines of responsibility for management control of the same components of costs?

244. Are data elements reconcilable between internal summary reports and reports forwarded to us?

245. Changes in the current direct and Assertive Community Treatment projected base?

246. Evaluate the performance of operating organizations?

247. Changes in the overhead pool and/or organization structures?

248. Are procedures established to prevent changes to the contract budget base other than the already stated authorized by contractual action?

249. Incurrence of actual indirect costs in excess of budgets, by element of expense?

250. The total budget for the contract (including estimates for authorized and unpriced work)?

251. Is authorization of budgets in excess of the contract budget base controlled formally and done with the full knowledge and recognition of the procuring activity?

252. Does the accounting system provide a basis for auditing records of direct costs chargeable to the contract?

253. Does the scheduling system provide for the identification of work progress against technical and other milestones, and also provide for forecasts of completion dates of scheduled work?

254. Are retroactive changes to direct costs and indirect costs prohibited except for the correction of errors and routine accounting adjustments?

255. What size should a work package be?

256. Are overhead costs budgets established on a basis consistent with anticipated direct business

base?

2.10 Schedule Management Plan: Assertive Community Treatment

257. Is the plan consistent with industry best practices?

258. Is there a formal set of procedures supporting Issues Management?

259. What will be the format of the schedule model?

260. Has a capability assessment been conducted?

261. Is a process defined for baseline approval and control?

262. Has the budget been baselined?

263. Are meeting objectives identified for each meeting?

264. Has a quality assurance plan been developed for the Assertive Community Treatment project?

265. Have Assertive Community Treatment project team accountabilities & responsibilities been clearly defined?

266. Staffing Requirements?

267. Are schedule performance measures defined including pre-set triggers for specific actions?

268. Is the quality assurance team identified?

269. Are the payment terms being followed?

270. Are cause and effect determined for risks when they occur?

271. Are the predecessor and successor relationships accurate?

272. Are assumptions being identified, recorded, analyzed, qualified and closed?

273. Are there checklists created to determine if all quality processes are followed?

274. Is there a procedure for management, control and release of schedule margin?

275. Are risk oriented checklists used during risk identification?

276. Are the activity durations realistic and at an appropriate level of detail for effective management?

2.11 Activity List: Assertive Community Treatment

277. What went well?

278. Is infrastructure setup part of your Assertive Community Treatment project?

279. How will it be performed?

280. How do you determine the late start (LS) for each activity?

281. Who will perform the work?

282. How difficult will it be to do specific activities on this Assertive Community Treatment project?

283. Where will it be performed?

284. Are the required resources available or need to be acquired?

285. What will be performed?

286. What went wrong?

287. How much slack is available in the Assertive Community Treatment project?

288. What is the probability the Assertive Community Treatment project can be completed in xx weeks?

289. The wbs is developed as part of a joint planning session. and how do you know that youhave done this right?

290. How detailed should a Assertive Community Treatment project get?

291. How can the Assertive Community Treatment project be displayed graphically to better visualize the activities?

292. When will the work be performed?

293. Is there anything planned that does not need to be here?

294. What is the LF and LS for each activity?

295. What did not go as well?

296. What is your organizations history in doing similar activities?

2.12 Activity Attributes: Assertive Community Treatment

297. Activity: what is In the Bag?

298. Is there a trend during the year?

299. What conclusions/generalizations can you draw from this?

300. Has management defined a definite timeframe for the turnaround or Assertive Community Treatment project window?

301. Were there other ways you could have organized the data to achieve similar results?

302. Do you feel very comfortable with your prediction?

303. Where else does it apply?

304. What is the general pattern here?

305. What activity do you think you should spend the most time on?

306. Resource is assigned to?

307. Can more resources be added?

308. Why?

309. Would you consider either of corresponding activities an outlier?

310. Activity: fair or not fair?

311. Resources to accomplish the work?

312. Does your organization of the data change its meaning?

313. How many days do you need to complete the work scope with a limit of X number of resources?

2.13 Milestone List: Assertive Community Treatment

314. Global influences?

315. Loss of key staff?

316. What are your competitors vulnerabilities?

317. Usps (unique selling points)?

318. How will the milestone be verified?

319. Describe your organizations strengths and core competencies. What factors will make your organization succeed?

320. How late can the activity start?

321. How soon can the activity start?

322. How late can each activity be finished and started?

323. Identify critical paths (one or more) and which activities are on the critical path?

324. What date will the task finish?

325. Which path is the critical path?

326. When will the Assertive Community Treatment project be complete?

327. Legislative effects?

328. Sustaining internal capabilities?

329. Reliability of data, plan predictability?

330. Marketing - reach, distribution, awareness?

331. Information and research?

2.14 Network Diagram: Assertive Community Treatment

332. Exercise: what is the probability that the Assertive Community Treatment project duration will exceed xx weeks?

333. What activity must be completed immediately before this activity can start?

334. How difficult will it be to do specific activities on this Assertive Community Treatment project?

335. What is the lowest cost to complete this Assertive Community Treatment project in xx weeks?

336. Planning: who, how long, what to do?

337. Are you on time?

338. How confident can you be in your milestone dates and the delivery date?

339. Which type of network diagram allows you to depict four types of dependencies?

340. Will crashing x weeks return more in benefits than it costs?

341. What must be completed before an activity can be started?

342. What activities must follow this activity?

343. Why must you schedule milestones, such as reviews, throughout the Assertive Community Treatment project?

344. What activities must occur simultaneously with this activity?

345. If the Assertive Community Treatment project network diagram cannot change and you have extra personnel resources, what is the BEST thing to do?

346. What can be done concurrently?

347. What controls the start and finish of a job?

348. What are the Major Administrative Issues?

349. What job or jobs could run concurrently?

350. What job or jobs precede it?

2.15 Activity Resource Requirements: Assertive Community Treatment

351. Why do you do that?

352. What are constraints that you might find during the Human Resource Planning process?

353. How do you handle petty cash?

354. How do you manage time?

355. How many signatures do you require on a check and does this match what is in your policy and procedures?

356. Organizational Applicability?

357. What is the Work Plan Standard?

358. Are there unresolved issues that need to be addressed?

359. Other support in specific areas?

360. When does monitoring begin?

361. Anything else?

362. Do you use tools like decomposition and rolling-wave planning to produce the activity list and other outputs?

363. Which logical relationship does the PDM use most often?

364. Time for overtime?

2.16 Resource Breakdown Structure: Assertive Community Treatment

365. The list could probably go on, but, the thing that you would most like to know is, How long & How much?

366. How can this help you with team building?

367. Why do you do it?

368. What is the purpose of assigning and documenting responsibility?

369. Who will be used as a Assertive Community Treatment project team member?

370. Who is allowed to see what data about which resources?

371. Who is allowed to perform which functions?

372. Who delivers the information?

373. What is the difference between % Complete and % work?

374. What are the requirements for resource data?

375. How difficult will it be to do specific activities on this Assertive Community Treatment project?

376. Why is this important?

377. When do they need the information?

378. What is the primary purpose of the human resource plan?

379. What is each stakeholders desired outcome for the Assertive Community Treatment project?

380. Which resource planning tool provides information on resource responsibility and accountability?

381. Which resources should be in the resource pool?

382. What defines a successful Assertive Community Treatment project?

2.17 Activity Duration Estimates: Assertive Community Treatment

383. Are performance reviews conducted regularly to assess the status of Assertive Community Treatment projects?

384. Total slack can be calculated by which equations?

385. What are the largest companies that provide information technology outsourcing services?

386. Are Assertive Community Treatment project management tools and techniques consistently applied throughout all Assertive Community Treatment projects?

387. What are some crucial elements of a good Assertive Community Treatment project plan?

388. Are time, scope, cost, and quality monitored throughout the Assertive Community Treatment project?

389. When would a milestone chart be used instead of a bar char?

390. Briefly describe some key events in the history of Assertive Community Treatment project management. What Assertive Community Treatment project was the first to use modern Assertive Community Treatment project management?

391. Do procedures exist describing how the Assertive Community Treatment project scope will be managed?

392. Are operational definitions created to identify quality measurement criteria for specific activities?

393. Are risks monitored to determine if an event has occurred or if the mitigation was successful?

394. Why do you need a good WBS to use Assertive Community Treatment project management software?

395. Assertive Community Treatment project has three critical paths. Which BEST describes how this affects the Assertive Community Treatment project?

396. Are changes to the scope managed according to defined procedures?

397. What is the duration of a milestone?

398. After how many days will the lease cost be the same as the purchase cost for the equipment?

399. Do you agree with the suggestions provided for improving Assertive Community Treatment project communications?

400. Why time management?

401. Why do you think schedule issues often cause the most conflicts on Assertive Community Treatment projects?

402. Consider the common sources of risk on information technology Assertive Community Treatment projects and suggestions for managing them. Which suggestions do you find most useful?

2.18 Duration Estimating Worksheet: Assertive Community Treatment

403. Done before proceeding with this activity or what can be done concurrently?

404. What is next?

405. For other activities, how much delay can be tolerated?

406. Will the Assertive Community Treatment project collaborate with the local community and leverage resources?

407. What questions do you have?

408. How can the Assertive Community Treatment project be displayed graphically to better visualize the activities?

409. What is the total time required to complete the Assertive Community Treatment project if no delays occur?

410. Does the Assertive Community Treatment project provide innovative ways for stakeholders to overcome obstacles or deliver better outcomes?

411. What info is needed?

412. What is an Average Assertive Community Treatment project?

413. What are the critical bottleneck activities?

414. Small or large Assertive Community Treatment project?

415. Define the work as completely as possible. What work will be included in the Assertive Community Treatment project?

416. How should ongoing costs be monitored to try to keep the Assertive Community Treatment project within budget?

417. When does your organization expect to be able to complete it?

418. Is a construction detail attached (to aid in explanation)?

419. What utility impacts are there?

420. Can the Assertive Community Treatment project be constructed as planned?

2.19 Project Schedule: Assertive Community Treatment

421. How can slack be negative?

422. Schedule/cost recovery?

423. What documents, if any, will the subcontractor provide (eg Assertive Community Treatment project schedule, quality plan etc)?

424. Change management required?

425. Your Assertive Community Treatment project management plan results in a Assertive Community Treatment project schedule that is too long. If the Assertive Community Treatment project network diagram cannot change and you have extra personnel resources, what is the BEST thing to do?

426. It allows the Assertive Community Treatment project to be delivered on schedule. How Do you Use Schedules?

427. How do you know that youhave done this right?

428. Are all remaining durations correct?

429. Should you include sub-activities?

430. Why is this particularly bad?

431. Is Assertive Community Treatment project work

proceeding in accordance with the original Assertive Community Treatment project schedule?

432. Why do you need schedules?

433. Activity charts and bar charts are graphical representations of a Assertive Community Treatment project schedule ...how do they differ?

434. What is the purpose of a Assertive Community Treatment project schedule?

435. Are procedures defined by which the Assertive Community Treatment project schedule may be changed?

436. Is there a Schedule Management Plan that establishes the criteria and activities for developing, monitoring and controlling the Assertive Community Treatment project schedule?

437. What is the difference?

438. Are activities connected because logic dictates the order in which others occur?

439. What is the most mis-scheduled part of process?

2.20 Cost Management Plan: Assertive Community Treatment

440. Are tasks tracked by hours?

441. Is there a formal set of procedures supporting Stakeholder Management?

442. Has the Assertive Community Treatment project scope been baselined?

443. Has the Assertive Community Treatment project manager been identified?

444. What is your organizations history in doing similar tasks?

445. Have process improvement efforts been completed before requirements efforts begin?

446. Do Assertive Community Treatment project managers participating in the Assertive Community Treatment project know the Assertive Community Treatment projects true status first hand?

447. Cost tracking and performance analysis - How will cost tracking and performance analysis be accomplished?

448. Are any non-compliance issues that exist due to State practices communicated to your organization?

449. Cost estimate preparation - What cost estimates

will be prepared during the Assertive Community Treatment project phases?

450. Were the budget estimates reasonable?

451. Was your organizations estimating methodology being used and followed?

452. What strengths do you have?

453. Does the Assertive Community Treatment project have a Statement of Work?

454. Are multiple estimation methods being employed?

455. Have Assertive Community Treatment project team accountabilities & responsibilities been clearly defined?

456. Have lessons learned been conducted after each Assertive Community Treatment project release?

2.21 Activity Cost Estimates: Assertive Community Treatment

457. Were sponsors and decision makers available when needed outside regularly scheduled meetings?

458. Can you delete activities or make them inactive?

459. Is costing method consistent with study goals?

460. Did the consultant work with local staff to develop local capacity?

461. How do you manage cost?

462. What is the activity inventory?

463. How do you fund change orders?

464. Were the costs or charges reasonable?

465. Will you need to provide essential services information about activities?

466. Who determines when the contractor is paid?

467. Is there anything unique in this Assertive Community Treatment projects scope statement that will affect resources?

468. What happens if you cannot produce the documentation for the single audit?

469. Certification of actual expenditures?

470. How difficult will it be to do specific tasks on the Assertive Community Treatment project?

471. What makes a good activity description?

472. How do you allocate indirect costs to activities?

473. Who determines the quality and expertise of contractors?

474. Were decisions made in a timely manner?

2.22 Cost Estimating Worksheet: Assertive Community Treatment

475. Will the Assertive Community Treatment project collaborate with the local community and leverage resources?

476. Identify the timeframe necessary to monitor progress and collect data to determine how the selected measure has changed?

477. Is the Assertive Community Treatment project responsive to community need?

478. How will the results be shared and to whom?

479. Is it feasible to establish a control group arrangement?

480. What costs are to be estimated?

481. What additional Assertive Community Treatment project(s) could be initiated as a result of this Assertive Community Treatment project?

482. What can be included?

483. Ask: are others positioned to know, are others credible, and will others cooperate?

484. Who is best positioned to know and assist in identifying corresponding factors?

485. What happens to any remaining funds not used?

486. Does the Assertive Community Treatment project provide innovative ways for stakeholders to overcome obstacles or deliver better outcomes?

487. What is the purpose of estimating?

488. Can a trend be established from historical performance data on the selected measure and are the criteria for using trend analysis or forecasting methods met?

489. What is the estimated labor cost today based upon this information?

490. What will others want?

491. Value pocket identification & quantification what are value pockets?

2.23 Cost Baseline: Assertive Community Treatment

492. Where do changes come from?

493. Review your risk triggers -have your risks changed?

494. What is the reality?

495. How likely is it to go wrong?

496. Does it impact schedule, cost, quality?

497. What is cost and Assertive Community Treatment project cost management?

498. How difficult will it be to do specific tasks on the Assertive Community Treatment project?

499. Definition of done can be traced back to the definitions of what are you providing to the customer in terms of deliverables?

500. Is the cr within Assertive Community Treatment project scope?

501. What threats might prevent you from getting there?

502. How will cost estimates be used?

503. Have the lessons learned been filed with the

Assertive Community Treatment project Management Office?

504. On time?

505. Why do you manage cost?

506. How concrete were original objectives?

507. Are there contingencies or conditions related to the acceptance?

508. Are you asking management for something as a result of this update?

509. Does a process exist for establishing a cost baseline to measure Assertive Community Treatment project performance?

510. Has the Assertive Community Treatment projected annual cost to operate and maintain the product(s) or service(s) been approved and funded?

511. Are you meeting with your team regularly?

2.24 Quality Management Plan: Assertive Community Treatment

512. How is staff trained?

513. Who gets results of work?

514. What are your organizations current levels and trends for the already stated measures related to employee wellbeing, satisfaction, and development?

515. Is a component/condition present?

516. Is it necessary?

517. Are you following the quality standards?

518. Methodology followed?

519. How does your organization address regulatory, legal, and ethical compliance?

520. Contradictory information between document sections?

521. Who is responsible for approving the qapp?

522. Are there processes in place to ensure internal consistency between the source code components?

523. Who is responsible?

524. Who is approving the QAPP?

525. Does a documented Assertive Community Treatment project organizational policy & plan (i.e. governance model) exist?

526. How does training support what is important to your organization and the individual?

527. Checking the completeness and appropriateness of the sampling and testing. Were the right locations/ samples tested for the right parameters?

528. Do you periodically review your data quality system to see that it is up to date and appropriate?

529. Do trained quality assurance auditors conduct the audits as defined in the Quality Management Plan and scheduled by the Assertive Community Treatment project manager?

530. Are there trends or hot spots?

2.25 Quality Metrics: Assertive Community Treatment

531. Is material complete (and does it meet the standards)?

532. What are your organizations next steps?

533. What level of statistical confidence do you use?

534. What forces exist that would cause them to change?

535. Was material distributed on time?

536. What is the timeline to meet your goal?

537. Is quality culture a competitive advantage?

538. There are many reasons to shore up quality-related metrics, and what metrics are important?

539. How should customers provide input?

540. What method of measurement do you use?

541. Where is quality now?

542. What approved evidence based screening tools can be used?

543. Are interface issues coordinated?

544. If the defect rate during testing is substantially higher than that of the previous release (or a similar product), then ask: Did you plan for and actually improve testing effectiveness?

545. Who is willing to lead?

546. How do you know if everyone is trying to improve the right things?

547. Which are the right metrics to use?

548. How are requirements conflicts resolved?

549. What documentation is required?

550. Who notifies stakeholders of normal and abnormal results?

2.26 Process Improvement Plan: Assertive Community Treatment

551. Has the time line required to move measurement results from the points of collection to databases or users been established?

552. Does your process ensure quality?

553. Why do you want to achieve the goal?

554. The motive is determined by asking, Why do you want to achieve this goal?

555. Have the supporting tools been developed or acquired?

556. To elicit goal statements, do you ask a question such as, What do you want to achieve?

557. How do you manage quality?

558. What personnel are the change agents for your initiative?

559. What personnel are the coaches for your initiative?

560. Are you making progress on your improvement plan?

561. Where do you focus?

562. Have the frequency of collection and the points in the process where measurements will be made been determined?

563. Are you making progress on the goals?

564. How do you measure?

565. Has a process guide to collect the data been developed?

566. What makes people good SPI coaches?

567. Where do you want to be?

568. What personnel are the champions for the initiative?

2.27 Responsibility Assignment Matrix: Assertive Community Treatment

569. What materials and procurements needed?

570. Do work packages consist of discrete tasks which are adequately described?

571. No rs: if a task has no one listed as responsible, who is getting the job done?

572. How do you manage remotely to staff in other Divisions?

573. Who is responsible for work and budgets for each wbs?

574. The anticipated business volume?

575. Is it safe to say you can handle more work or that some tasks you are supposed to do arent worth doing?

576. Too many rs: with too many people labeled as doing the work, are there too many hands involved?

577. What are the known stakeholder requirements?

578. Changes in the current direct and Assertive Community Treatment projected base?

579. How do you manage human resources?

580. Are the requirements for all items of overhead established by rational, traceable processes?

581. Is accountability placed at the lowest-possible level within the Assertive Community Treatment project so that decisions can be made at that level?

582. What do you do when people do not respond?

583. With too many people labeled as doing the work, are there too many hands involved?

584. Detailed schedules which support control account and work package start and completion dates/events?

585. What do you need to implement earned value management?

586. Evaluate the impact of schedule changes, work around, etc?

2.28 Roles and Responsibilities: Assertive Community Treatment

587. Who is responsible for implementation activities and where will the functions, roles and responsibilities be defined?

588. Concern: where are you limited or have no authority, where you can not influence?

589. Are your policies supportive of a culture of quality data?

590. Was the expectation clearly communicated?

591. Who is involved?

592. What expectations were NOT met?

593. Are Assertive Community Treatment project team roles and responsibilities identified and documented?

594. Accountabilities: what are the roles and responsibilities of individual team members?

595. Key conclusions and recommendations: Are conclusions and recommendations relevant and acceptable?

596. To decide whether to use a quality measurement, ask how will you know when it is achieved?

597. Is feedback clearly communicated and non-

judgmental?

598. Are the quality assurance functions and related roles and responsibilities clearly defined?

599. Once the responsibilities are defined for the Assertive Community Treatment project, have the deliverables, roles and responsibilities been clearly communicated to every participant?

600. What specific behaviors did you observe?

601. Are your budgets supportive of a culture of quality data?

602. Are Assertive Community Treatment project team roles and responsibilities identified and documented?

603. What should you highlight for improvement?

604. Required skills, knowledge, experience?

605. Who is responsible for each task?

606. Implementation of actions: Who are the responsible units?

2.29 Human Resource Management Plan: Assertive Community Treatment

607. Do Assertive Community Treatment project teams & team members report on status / activities / progress?

608. How to convince employees that this is a necessary process?

609. Are the Assertive Community Treatment project team members located locally to the users/ stakeholders?

610. Is there an issues management plan in place?

611. Is your organization heading towards expansion, outsourcing of certain talents or making cut-backs to save money?

612. Is quality monitored from the perspective of the customers needs and expectations?

613. Based on your Assertive Community Treatment project communication management plan, what worked well?

614. Have all documents been archived in a Assertive Community Treatment project repository for each release?

615. Has a sponsor been identified?

616. Are mitigation strategies identified?

617. Quality of people required to meet the forecast needs of the department?

618. Are all payments made according to the contract(s)?

619. What were things that you did well, and could improve, and how?

620. Are internal Assertive Community Treatment project status meetings held at reasonable intervals?

621. Who is evaluated?

622. Responsiveness to change and the resulting demands for different skills and abilities?

623. Have Assertive Community Treatment project management standards and procedures been identified / established and documented?

624. Has the Assertive Community Treatment project scope been baselined?

625. Have all involved Assertive Community Treatment project stakeholders and work groups committed to the Assertive Community Treatment project?

2.30 Communications Management Plan: Assertive Community Treatment

626. Are you constantly rushing from meeting to meeting?

627. How often do you engage with stakeholders?

628. Will messages be directly related to the release strategy or phases of the Assertive Community Treatment project?

629. Are there potential barriers between the team and the stakeholder?

630. Is there an important stakeholder who is actively opposed and will not receive messages?

631. What communications method?

632. Who to learn from?

633. What is the stakeholders level of authority?

634. Who have you worked with in past, similar initiatives?

635. What is the political influence?

636. Are there common objectives between the team and the stakeholder?

637. What are the interrelationships?

638. What to learn?

639. How were corresponding initiatives successful?

640. Who will use or be affected by the result of a Assertive Community Treatment project?

641. What does the stakeholder need from the team?

642. Can you think of other people who might have concerns or interests?

643. How is this initiative related to other portfolios, programs, or Assertive Community Treatment projects?

644. Are others needed?

2.31 Risk Management Plan: Assertive Community Treatment

645. Does the Assertive Community Treatment project team have experience with the technology to be implemented?

646. Are the metrics meaningful and useful?

647. For software; are compilers and code generators available and suitable for the product to be built?

648. How is risk response planning performed?

649. Risks should be identified during which phase of Assertive Community Treatment project management life cycle?

650. Market risk -will the new service or product be useful to your organization or marketable to others?

651. Does the Assertive Community Treatment project have the authority and ability to avoid the risk?

652. Is this an issue, action item, question or a risk?

653. Where are you confronted with risks during the business phases?

654. Have staff received necessary training?

655. Are end-users enthusiastically committed to the Assertive Community Treatment project and the

system/product to be built?

656. Are team members trained in the use of the tools?

657. Are people attending meetings and doing work?

658. Are you on schedule?

659. How is the audit profession changing?

660. Risk probability and impact: how will the probabilities and impacts of risk items be assessed?

661. User involvement: do you have the right users?

662. What will the damage be?

663. Is the customer willing to establish rapid communication links with the developer?

664. Which risks should get the attention?

2.32 Risk Register: Assertive Community Treatment

665. What are your key risks/show istoppers and what is being done to manage them?

666. Methodology: how will risk management be performed on this Assertive Community Treatment project?

667. Recovery actions - planned actions taken once a risk has occurred to allow you to move on. What should you do after?

668. What is the appropriate level of risk management for this Assertive Community Treatment project?

669. Amongst the action plans and recommendations that you have to introduce are there some that could stop or delay the overall program?

670. What would the impact to the Assertive Community Treatment project objectives be should the risk arise?

671. When is it going to be done?

672. Assume the risk event or situation happens, what would the impact be?

673. Risk categories: what are the main categories of risks that should be addressed on this Assertive Community Treatment project?

674. Who is going to do it?

675. Who is accountable?

676. What could prevent you delivering on the strategic program objectives and what is being done to mitigate corresponding issues?

677. Preventative actions - planned actions to reduce the likelihood a risk will occur and/or reduce the seriousness should it occur. What should you do now?

678. Schedule impact/severity estimated range (workdays) assume the event happens, what is the potential impact?

679. What is a Community Risk Register?

680. How could corresponding Risk affect the Assertive Community Treatment project in terms of cost and schedule?

681. What are the assumptions and current status that support the assessment of the risk?

682. What is the reason for current performance gaps and do the risks and opportunities identified previously account for this?

2.33 Probability and Impact Assessment: Assertive Community Treatment

683. My Assertive Community Treatment project leader has suddenly left your organization, what do you do?

684. Workarounds are determined during which step of risk management?

685. What risks are necessary to achieve success?

686. What kind of preparation would be required to do this?

687. Mitigation -how can you avoid the risk?

688. What is the likelihood of a breakthrough?

689. How do risks change during a Assertive Community Treatment project life cycle?

690. Who will be in command to monitor and control the performance of the consortium members (consortium leader/client)?

691. What are the chances the event will occur?

692. Has the need for the Assertive Community Treatment project been properly established?

693. How are the local factors going to affect the

absorption?

694. What are the channels available for distribution to the customer?

695. Should the risk be taken at all?

696. Are testing tools available and suitable?

697. What should be the external organizations responsibility vis-à-vis total stake in the Assertive Community Treatment project?

698. Do the people have the right combinations of skills?

699. What are the preparations required for facing difficulties?

700. Risk categorization -which of your categories has more risk than others?

701. Assuming that you have identified a number of risks in the Assertive Community Treatment project, how would you prioritize them?

2.34 Probability and Impact Matrix: Assertive Community Treatment

702. Can you stabilize dynamic risk factors?

703. How will the consumption pattern change?

704. How risk averse are you?

705. Is a software Assertive Community Treatment project management tool available?

706. Are the software tools integrated with each other?

707. Degree of confidence in estimated size estimate?

708. How completely has the customer been identified?

709. Is the delay in one subAssertive Community Treatment project going to affect another?

710. Can it be enlarged by drawing people from other areas of your organization?

711. Is the process supported by tools?

712. How is the risk management process used in practice?

713. Are some people working on multiple Assertive Community Treatment projects?

714. What are ways to measure and evaluate risks?

715. What is the culture of the market and your organization?

716. If you can not fix it, how do you do it differently?

717. What is the likelihood?

718. What is your anticipated volatility of the requirements?

719. Which of the risk factors can be avoided altogether?

720. Have you ascribed a level of confidence to every critical technical objective?

2.35 Risk Data Sheet: Assertive Community Treatment

721. What is the likelihood of it happening?

722. What was measured?

723. What will be the consequences if it happens?

724. Are new hazards created?

725. What is the environment within which you operate (social trends, economic, community values, broad based participation, national directions etc.)?

726. Risk of what?

727. What are your core values?

728. What are the main opportunities available to you that you should grab while you can?

729. What were the Causes that contributed?

730. What actions can be taken to eliminate or remove risk?

731. What can you do?

732. Whom do you serve (customers)?

733. What are you trying to achieve (Objectives)?

734. Type of risk identified?

735. What if client refuses?

736. How reliable is the data source?

737. During work activities could hazards exist?

738. Will revised controls lead to tolerable risk levels?

2.36 Procurement Management Plan: Assertive Community Treatment

739. Is a payment system in place with proper reviews and approvals?

740. Does the Assertive Community Treatment project team have the right skills?

741. Published materials?

742. Is there a formal process for updating the Assertive Community Treatment project baseline?

743. Were Assertive Community Treatment project team members involved in detailed estimating and scheduling?

744. Are all key components of a Quality Assurance Plan present?

745. Are corrective actions and variances reported?

746. Are the Assertive Community Treatment project plans updated on a frequent basis?

747. Are the Assertive Community Treatment project team members located locally to the users/ stakeholders?

748. Is the steering committee active in Assertive Community Treatment project oversight?

749. Are change requests logged and managed?

750. Are trade-offs between accepting the risk and mitigating the risk identified?

751. Has the schedule been baselined?

752. Has a resource management plan been created?

753. Are vendor invoices audited for accuracy before payment?

754. Is Assertive Community Treatment project status reviewed with the steering and executive teams at appropriate intervals?

2.37 Source Selection Criteria: Assertive Community Treatment

755. Does an evaluation need to include the identification of strengths and weaknesses?

756. Are they compliant with all technical requirements?

757. Do you want to have them collaborate at subfactor level?

758. How organization are proposed quotes/prices?

759. In the technical/management area, what criteria do you use to determine the final evaluation ratings?

760. How do you consolidate reviews and analysis of evaluators?

761. Who must be notified?

762. Is the contracting office likely to receive more purchase requests for this item or service during the coming year?

763. Are resultant proposal revisions allowed?

764. How should the solicitation aspects regarding past performance be structured?

765. What should be considered?

766. Are there any common areas of weaknesses or deficiencies in the proposals in the competitive range?

767. How important is cost in the source selection decision relative to past performance and technical considerations?

768. How will you decide an evaluators write up is sufficient?

769. Does the evaluation of any change include an impact analysis; how will the change affect the scope, time, cost, and quality of the goods or services being provided?

770. When is it appropriate to conduct a preproposal conference?

771. How can business terms and conditions be improved to yield more effective price competition?

772. What is the last item a Assertive Community Treatment project manager must do to finalize Assertive Community Treatment project close-out?

773. Will the technical evaluation factor unnecessarily force the acquisition into a higher-priced market segment?

774. Who is on the Source Selection Advisory Committee?

2.38 Stakeholder Management Plan: Assertive Community Treatment

775. Are the people assigned to the Assertive Community Treatment project sufficiently qualified?

776. Are Assertive Community Treatment project team members committed fulltime?

777. Does a documented Assertive Community Treatment project organizational policy & plan (i.e. governance model) exist?

778. What is the difference between product and Assertive Community Treatment project scope?

779. If a problem has been detected, what tools can be used to determine a root cause?

780. Were Assertive Community Treatment project team members involved in the development of activity & task decomposition?

781. Is there a formal process for updating the Assertive Community Treatment project baseline?

782. Is the communication plan being followed?

783. What methods are to be used for managing and monitoring subcontractors (eg agreements, contracts etc)?

784. What preventative action can be taken to reduce

the likelihood a risk will be realised?

785. How, to whom and how frequently will Risk status be reported?

786. Do Assertive Community Treatment project managers participating in the Assertive Community Treatment project know the Assertive Community Treatment projects true status first hand?

787. Was trending evident between audits?

788. Why would you develop a Assertive Community Treatment project Execution Plan?

789. Are formal code reviews conducted?

790. Where does the information come from?

791. What is the drawback in using qualitative Assertive Community Treatment project selection techniques?

2.39 Change Management Plan: Assertive Community Treatment

792. Readiness -what is a successful end state?

793. Who will fund the training?

794. What policies and procedures need to be changed?

795. What is the negative impact of communicating too soon or too late?

796. How does the principle of senders and receivers make the Assertive Community Treatment project communications effort more complex?

797. What is the reason for the communication?

798. Where will the funds come from?

799. Identify the risk and assess the significance and likelihood of it occurring and plan the contingency What risks may occur upfront?

800. How badly can information be misinterpreted?

801. Which relationships will change?

802. Who might present the most resistance?

803. What are the dependencies?

804. What are the training strategies?

805. Who might be able to help you the most?

806. Has the priority for this Assertive Community Treatment project been set by the Business Unit Management Team?

807. When to start change management?

808. What are the major changes to processes?

809. Are there any restrictions on who can receive the communications?

810. What time commitment will this involve?

3.0 Executing Process Group: Assertive Community Treatment

811. Based on your Assertive Community Treatment project communication management plan, what worked well?

812. How well did the chosen processes produce the expected results?

813. Does the case present a realistic scenario?

814. Measurable - are the targets measurable?

815. How do you enter durations, link tasks, and view critical path information?

816. If action is called for, what form should it take?

817. When is the appropriate time to bring the scorecard to Board meetings?

818. Do schedule issues conflicts?

819. Does the Assertive Community Treatment project team have enough people to execute the Assertive Community Treatment project plan?

820. What were things that you did very well and want to do the same again on the next Assertive Community Treatment project?

821. How could you control progress of your Assertive

Community Treatment project?

822. How does a Assertive Community Treatment project life cycle differ from a product life cycle?

823. What are the key components of the Assertive Community Treatment project communications plan?

824. Who are the Assertive Community Treatment project stakeholders?

825. How do you control progress of your Assertive Community Treatment project?

826. What is the difference between using brainstorming and the Delphi technique for risk identification?

827. Just how important is your work to the overall success of the Assertive Community Treatment project?

3.1 Team Member Status Report: Assertive Community Treatment

828. How much risk is involved?

829. How can you make it practical?

830. Does the product, good, or service already exist within your organization?

831. Are the products of your organizations Assertive Community Treatment projects meeting customers objectives?

832. Does your organization have the means (staff, money, contract, etc.) to produce or to acquire the product, good, or service?

833. Will the staff do training or is that done by a third party?

834. When a teams productivity and success depend on collaboration and the efficient flow of information, what generally fails them?

835. Does every department have to have a Assertive Community Treatment project Manager on staff?

836. The problem with Reward & Recognition Programs is that the truly deserving people all too often get left out. How can you make it practical?

837. What is to be done?

838. Are your organizations Assertive Community Treatment projects more successful over time?

839. Are the attitudes of staff regarding Assertive Community Treatment project work improving?

840. How does this product, good, or service meet the needs of the Assertive Community Treatment project and your organization as a whole?

841. How will resource planning be done?

842. How it is to be done?

843. Is there evidence that staff is taking a more professional approach toward management of your organizations Assertive Community Treatment projects?

844. Why is it to be done?

845. Do you have an Enterprise Assertive Community Treatment project Management Office (EPMO)?

846. What specific interest groups do you have in place?

3.2 Change Request: Assertive Community Treatment

847. Screen shots or attachments included in a Change Request?

848. What is the function of the change control committee?

849. How are changes requested (forms, method of communication)?

850. Will the change use memory to the extent that other functions will be not have sufficient memory to operate effectively?

851. How is the change documented (format, content, storage)?

852. How is quality being addressed on the Assertive Community Treatment project?

853. What is the relationship between requirements attributes and attributes like complexity and size?

854. When to submit a change request?

855. Will all change requests and current status be logged?

856. Who will perform the change?

857. What must be taken into consideration when

introducing change control programs?

858. Has your address changed?

859. Are you implementing itil processes?

860. Can you answer what happened, who did it, when did it happen, and what else will be affected?

861. Why were your requested changes rejected or not made?

862. How does your organization control changes before and after software is released to a customer?

863. Which requirements attributes affect the risk to reliability the most?

864. How well do experienced software developers predict software change?

865. What is the purpose of change control?

3.3 Change Log: Assertive Community Treatment

866. Is the requested change request a result of changes in other Assertive Community Treatment project(s)?

867. How does this change affect the timeline of the schedule?

868. Is the change request within Assertive Community Treatment project scope?

869. Do the described changes impact on the integrity or security of the system?

870. Should a more thorough impact analysis be conducted?

871. When was the request submitted?

872. Is this a mandatory replacement?

873. Who initiated the change request?

874. Does the suggested change request seem to represent a necessary enhancement to the product?

875. Is the submitted change a new change or a modification of a previously approved change?

876. How does this change affect scope?

877. Is the change request open, closed or pending?

878. How does this relate to the standards developed for specific business processes?

879. Is the change backward compatible without limitations?

880. When was the request approved?

881. Does the suggested change request represent a desired enhancement to the products functionality?

882. Will the Assertive Community Treatment project fail if the change request is not executed?

3.4 Decision Log: Assertive Community Treatment

883. At what point in time does loss become unacceptable?

884. Behaviors; what are guidelines that the team has identified that will assist them with getting the most out of team meetings?

885. It becomes critical to track and periodically revisit both operational effectiveness; Are you noticing all that you need to, and are you interpreting what you see effectively?

886. How does an increasing emphasis on cost containment influence the strategies and tactics used?

887. What was the rationale for the decision?

888. How effective is maintaining the log at facilitating organizational learning?

889. How consolidated and comprehensive a story can you tell by capturing currently available incident data in a central location and through a log of key decisions during an incident?

890. Which variables make a critical difference?

891. What is the line where eDiscovery ends and document review begins?

892. What is the average size of your matters in an applicable measurement?

893. What is your overall strategy for quality control / quality assurance procedures?

894. How does the use a Decision Support System influence the strategies/tactics or costs?

895. Adversarial environment. is your opponent open to a non-traditional workflow, or will it likely challenge anything you do?

896. Meeting purpose; why does this team meet?

897. What are the cost implications?

898. What alternatives/risks were considered?

899. Who will be given a copy of this document and where will it be kept?

900. Linked to original objective?

901. What makes you different or better than others companies selling the same thing?

902. How do you know when you are achieving it?

3.5 Quality Audit: Assertive Community Treatment

903. How does your organization know that its security arrangements are appropriately effective and constructive?

904. How does your organization know that its system for supporting staff research capability is appropriately effective and constructive?

905. Do prior clients have a positive opinion of your organization?

906. How does your organization know that its staff support services planning and management systems are appropriately effective and constructive?

907. How does your organization know that its Governance system is appropriately effective and constructive?

908. What are you trying to do?

909. How does your organization know that its system for ensuring a positive organizational climate is appropriately effective and constructive?

910. How does your organization know that its staff financial services are appropriately effective and constructive?

911. How does your organization know that its

financial management system is appropriately effective and constructive?

912. Can your organization demonstrate exactly how and why results were achieved?

913. Are training programs documented?

914. What are your supplier audits?

915. Is your organizations resource allocation system properly aligned with its collection of intentions?

916. Is there a written corporate quality policy?

917. What are the main things that hinder your ability to do a good job?

918. How does your organization know that its promotions system is appropriately effective, constructive and fair?

919. How does your organization know that its system for commercializing research outputs is appropriately effective and constructive?

920. Are all records associated with the reconditioning of a device maintained for a minimum of two years after the sale or disposal of the last device within a lot of merchandise?

921. How does your organization know that its support services planning and management systems are appropriately effective and constructive?

3.6 Team Directory: Assertive Community Treatment

922. Who should receive information (all stakeholders)?

923. Why is the work necessary?

924. Process decisions: how well was task order work performed?

925. Who will write the meeting minutes and distribute?

926. Timing: when do the effects of communication take place?

927. Who are the Team Members?

928. Have you decided when to celebrate the Assertive Community Treatment projects completion date?

929. What are you going to deliver or accomplish?

930. Process decisions: are all start-up, turn over and close out requirements of the contract satisfied?

931. How do unidentified risks impact the outcome of the Assertive Community Treatment project?

932. Process decisions: are contractors adequately prosecuting the work?

933. Who will be the stakeholders on your next Assertive Community Treatment project?

934. Where should the information be distributed?

935. Do purchase specifications and configurations match requirements?

936. Contract requirements complied with?

937. Who will talk to the customer?

938. Process decisions: do invoice amounts match accepted work in place?

939. Process decisions: is work progressing on schedule and per contract requirements?

940. How will you accomplish and manage the objectives?

3.7 Team Operating Agreement: Assertive Community Treatment

941. Are there differences in access to communication and collaboration technology based on team member location?

942. To whom do you deliver your services?

943. What types of accommodations will be formulated and put in place for sustaining the team?

944. Must your team members rely on the expertise of other members to complete tasks?

945. Did you prepare participants for the next meeting?

946. How will you resolve conflict efficiently and respectfully?

947. Does your team need access to all documents and information at all times?

948. What is the anticipated procedure (recruitment, solicitation of volunteers, or assignment) for selecting team members?

949. Have you set the goals and objectives of the team?

950. What is the number of cases currently teamed?

951. Do you begin with a question to engage everyone?

952. Do you determine the meeting length and time of day?

953. Are leadership responsibilities shared among team members (versus a single leader)?

954. What is group supervision?

955. Are there more than two functional areas represented by your team?

956. How will group handle unplanned absences?

957. What individual strengths does each team member bring to the group?

958. Are there influences outside the team that may affect performance, and if so, have you identified and addressed them?

959. Must your members collaborate successfully to complete Assertive Community Treatment projects?

3.8 Team Performance Assessment: Assertive Community Treatment

960. To what degree does the teams work approach provide opportunity for members to engage in fact-based problem solving?

961. To what degree does the teams purpose contain themes that are particularly meaningful and memorable?

962. Where to from here?

963. Do you give group members authority to make at least some important decisions?

964. When does the medium matter?

965. To what degree can all members engage in open and interactive considerations?

966. To what degree are sub-teams possible or necessary?

967. To what degree are corresponding categories of skills either actually or potentially represented across the membership?

968. Individual task proficiency and team process behavior: what is important for team functioning?

969. What are teams?

970. To what degree are staff involved as partners in the improvement process?

971. If you have criticized someones work for method variance in your role as reviewer, what was the circumstance?

972. What makes opportunities more or less obvious?

973. Delaying market entry: how long is too long?

974. If you have received criticism from reviewers that your work suffered from method variance, what was the circumstance?

975. To what degree do members understand and articulate the same purpose without relying on ambiguous abstractions?

976. To what degree is there a sense that only the team can succeed?

977. Social categorization and intergroup behaviour: Does minimal intergroup discrimination make social identity more positive?

978. Which situations call for a more extreme type of adaptiveness in which team members actually re-define roles?

979. How do you keep key people outside the group informed about its accomplishments?

3.9 Team Member Performance Assessment: Assertive Community Treatment

980. How often are assessments to be conducted?

981. Do the goals support your organizations goals?

982. What variables that affect team members achievement are within your control?

983. Has the appropriate access to relevant data and analysis capability been granted?

984. What stakeholders must be involved in the development and oversight of the performance plan?

985. To what degree is the team cognizant of small wins to be celebrated along the way?

986. How is assessment information achieved, stored?

987. To what degree can the team measure progress against specific goals?

988. Can your organization rate by exception and assume that most employees are performing at an acceptable level?

989. What evaluation results did you have?

990. What happens if a team member receives a Rating of Unsatisfactory?

991. To what degree are the teams goals and objectives clear, simple, and measurable?

992. How was the determination made for which training platforms would be used (i.e., media selection)?

993. How is performance assessment used in making future award decisions including options and extend/compete decisions?

994. What are top priorities?

995. What are they responsible for?

996. To what degree do members articulate the goals beyond the team membership?

997. Does statute or regulation require the job responsibility?

3.10 Issue Log: Assertive Community Treatment

998. Do you often overlook a key stakeholder or stakeholder group?

999. Are there too many who have an interest in some aspect of your work?

1000. What date was the issue resolved?

1001. How do you manage communications?

1002. Can an impact cause deviation beyond team, stage or Assertive Community Treatment project tolerances?

1003. In classifying stakeholders, which approach to do so are you using?

1004. Is access to the Issue Log controlled?

1005. What effort will a change need?

1006. Why not more evaluators?

1007. Who are the members of the governing body?

1008. Where do team members get information?

1009. What approaches to you feel are the best ones to use?

1010. Why do you manage communications?

1011. Do you have members of your team responsible for certain stakeholders?

1012. Do you feel more overwhelmed by stakeholders?

1013. What are the typical contents?

1014. Persistence; will users learn a work around or will they be bothered every time?

1015. Who reported the issue?

4.0 Monitoring and Controlling Process Group: Assertive Community Treatment

1016. Is progress on outcomes due to your program?

1017. Did you implement the program as designed?

1018. How well did you do?

1019. Is there sufficient funding available for this?

1020. What good practices or successful experiences or transferable examples have been identified?

1021. How is agile portfolio management done?

1022. How to ensure validity, quality and consistency?

1023. Did the Assertive Community Treatment project team have enough people to execute the Assertive Community Treatment project plan?

1024. User: who wants the information and what are they interested in?

1025. How is agile program management done?

1026. In what way has the program come up with innovative measures for problem-solving?

1027. Is there sufficient time allotted between the general system design and the detailed system design phases?

1028. What is the timeline?

1029. What communication items need improvement?

1030. How were collaborations developed, and how are they sustained?

1031. What is the expected monetary value of the Assertive Community Treatment project?

1032. Is it what was agreed upon?

4.1 Project Performance Report: Assertive Community Treatment

1033. To what degree can team members vigorously define the teams purpose in considerations with others who are not part of the functioning team?

1034. To what degree do individual skills and abilities match task demands?

1035. To what degree are the structures of the formal organization consistent with the behaviors in the informal organization?

1036. What degree are the relative importance and priority of the goals clear to all team members?

1037. To what degree are the tasks requirements reflected in the flow and storage of information?

1038. To what degree is the information network consistent with the structure of the formal organization?

1039. To what degree does the task meet individual needs?

1040. To what degree will team members, individually and collectively, commit time to help themselves and others learn and develop skills?

1041. To what degree will new and supplemental skills be introduced as the need is recognized?

1042. To what degree do team members feel that the purpose of the team is important, if not exciting?

1043. To what degree does the informal organization make use of individual resources and meet individual needs?

1044. To what degree is there centralized control of information sharing?

1045. To what degree are the members clear on what they are individually responsible for and what they are jointly responsible for?

1046. To what degree does the funding match the requirement?

1047. Next Steps?

4.2 Variance Analysis: Assertive Community Treatment

1048. Is there a logical explanation for any variance?

1049. How are variances affected by multiple material and labor categories?

1050. Are meaningful indicators identified for use in measuring the status of cost and schedule performance?

1051. Is cost and schedule performance measurement done in a consistent, systematic manner?

1052. What are the actual costs to date?

1053. Why are standard cost systems used?

1054. Do you identify potential or actual budget-based and time-based schedule variances?

1055. Are all cwbs elements specified for external reporting?

1056. What does a favorable labor efficiency variance mean?

1057. Are the bases and rates for allocating costs from each indirect pool consistently applied?

1058. Does the contractor use objective results, design reviews and tests to trace schedule performance?

1059. What is the actual cost of work performed?

1060. How do you identify and isolate causes of favorable and unfavorable cost and schedule variances?

1061. What are the direct labor dollars and/or hours?

1062. Are there knowledgeable Assertive Community Treatment projections of future performance?

1063. What business event causes fluctuations?

1064. Did your organization lose existing customers and/or gain new customers?

1065. Are work packages assigned to performing organizations?

1066. Is work progressively subdivided into detailed work packages as requirements are defined?

1067. Are records maintained to show how undistributed budgets are controlled?

4.3 Earned Value Status: Assertive Community Treatment

1068. How much is it going to cost by the finish?

1069. Are you hitting your Assertive Community Treatment projects targets?

1070. When is it going to finish?

1071. Verification is a process of ensuring that the developed system satisfies the stakeholders agreements and specifications; Are you building the product right? What do you verify?

1072. What is the unit of forecast value?

1073. Earned value can be used in almost any Assertive Community Treatment project situation and in almost any Assertive Community Treatment project environment. it may be used on large Assertive Community Treatment projects, medium sized Assertive Community Treatment projects, tiny Assertive Community Treatment projects (in cut-down form), complex and simple Assertive Community Treatment projects and in any market sector. some people, of course, know all about earned value, they have used it for years - but perhaps not as effectively as they could have?

1074. Where are your problem areas?

1075. Validation is a process of ensuring that

the developed system will actually achieve the stakeholders desired outcomes; Are you building the right product? What do you validate?

1076. If earned value management (EVM) is so good in determining the true status of a Assertive Community Treatment project and Assertive Community Treatment project its completion, why is it that hardly any one uses it in information systems related Assertive Community Treatment projects?

1077. Where is evidence-based earned value in your organization reported?

1078. How does this compare with other Assertive Community Treatment projects?

4.4 Risk Audit: Assertive Community Treatment

1079. Risks with Assertive Community Treatment projects or new initiatives?

1080. Are audit program plans risk-adjusted?

1081. Is your organization willing to commit significant time to the requirements gathering process?

1082. Can analytical tests provide evidence that is as strong as evidence from traditional substantive tests?

1083. Do you conduct risk assessments on all programs, activities and events?

1084. Is all expenditure authorised through an identified process?

1085. Does the team have the right mix of skills?

1086. Do you have a procedure for dealing with complaints?

1087. Is Assertive Community Treatment project scope stable?

1088. What expertise do auditors need to generate effective business-level risk assessments, and to what extent do auditors currently possess the already stated attributes?

1089. What is the anticipated volatility of the requirements?

1090. What are the legal implications of not identifying a complete universe of business risks?

1091. Do all coaches/instructors/leaders have appropriate and current accreditation?

1092. Assessing risk with analytical procedures: do systemsthinking tools help auditors focus on diagnostic patterns?

1093. Does the customer understand the process?

1094. How do you compare to other jurisdictions when managing the risk of ....?

1095. Does your auditor understand your business?

1096. Can assurance be expanded beyond the traditional audit without undermining independence?

1097. How will you maximise opportunities?

1098. What limitations do auditors face in effectively applying risk-assessment results to the risk of material misstatement measures?

4.5 Contractor Status Report: Assertive Community Treatment

1099. How does the proposed individual meet each requirement?

1100. What was the actual budget or estimated cost for your organizations services?

1101. What was the budget or estimated cost for your organizations services?

1102. How is risk transferred?

1103. What is the average response time for answering a support call?

1104. What are the minimum and optimal bandwidth requirements for the proposed solution?

1105. What process manages the contracts?

1106. What was the overall budget or estimated cost?

1107. Who can list a Assertive Community Treatment project as organization experience, your organization or a previous employee of your organization?

1108. Describe how often regular updates are made to the proposed solution. Are corresponding regular updates included in the standard maintenance plan?

1109. If applicable; describe your standard schedule

for new software version releases. Are new software version releases included in the standard maintenance plan?

1110. How long have you been using the services?

1111. What was the final actual cost?

1112. Are there contractual transfer concerns?

4.6 Formal Acceptance: Assertive Community Treatment

1113. Do you perform formal acceptance or burn-in tests?

1114. Was the Assertive Community Treatment project managed well?

1115. Was the Assertive Community Treatment project work done on time, within budget, and according to specification?

1116. Did the Assertive Community Treatment project achieve its MOV?

1117. Was the sponsor/customer satisfied?

1118. What are the requirements against which to test, Who will execute?

1119. Who supplies data?

1120. What lessons were learned about your Assertive Community Treatment project management methodology?

1121. Was the client satisfied with the Assertive Community Treatment project results?

1122. What function(s) does it fill or meet?

1123. Was the Assertive Community Treatment project

goal achieved?

1124. What can you do better next time?

1125. What is the Acceptance Management Process?

1126. Is formal acceptance of the Assertive Community Treatment project product documented and distributed?

1127. Does it do what client said it would?

1128. Was business value realized?

1129. How well did the team follow the methodology?

1130. Do you buy-in installation services?

1131. Did the Assertive Community Treatment project manager and team act in a professional and ethical manner?

1132. What features, practices, and processes proved to be strengths or weaknesses?

5.0 Closing Process Group: Assertive Community Treatment

1133. What areas does the group agree are the biggest success on the Assertive Community Treatment project?

1134. Is this a follow-on to a previous Assertive Community Treatment project?

1135. Is the Assertive Community Treatment project funded?

1136. What were the actual outcomes?

1137. How well did the team follow the chosen processes?

1138. How dependent is the Assertive Community Treatment project on other Assertive Community Treatment projects or work efforts?

1139. What could be done to improve the process?

1140. Is this an updated Assertive Community Treatment project Proposal Document?

1141. Specific - is the objective clear in terms of what, how, when, and where the situation will be changed?

1142. What is the risk of failure to your organization?

1143. What do you need to do?

1144. Did you do what you said you were going to do?

1145. Will the Assertive Community Treatment project deliverable(s) replace a current asset or group of assets?

1146. How will staff learn how to use the deliverables?

1147. What were the desired outcomes?

1148. Did the Assertive Community Treatment project management methodology work?

1149. Were escalated issues resolved promptly?

1150. Just how important is your work to the overall success of the Assertive Community Treatment project?

5.1 Procurement Audit: Assertive Community Treatment

1151. Are risks managed to provide reasonable assurance regarding department procurement objectives?

1152. Are there procedures governing how sales and use tax will be handled (ordering in state versus ordering out of state)?

1153. Was the dynamic purchasing system set up following the rules of open procedure?

1154. Was additional significant information supplied to all interested parties?

1155. Are the number of checking accounts where cash segregation is not required kept to a reasonable number?

1156. Does your organization have an overall strategy and/or policy on public procurement, providing guidance for procuring entities?

1157. Was the outcome of the award process properly reached and communicated?

1158. Does the manual contain policies relating to all business management functions?

1159. Did the bidder comply with requests within the deadline set?

1160. Is the appropriate procurement approach being chosen (considering for example the possibility of contracting out work or procuring low value items through a specific low cost procuring system)?

1161. Are prices always included on the purchase order?

1162. Are there systems for recording and managing stocks (where part of contract)?

1163. Are all purchase orders accounted for?

1164. Was the performance description adequate to needs and legal requirements?

1165. Are all purchase orders reviewed by someone other than the individual preparing the purchase order (reasonableness of order and vendor selection)?

1166. Can small orders such as magazine subscriptions and non-product items such as membership in organizations be processed by the ordering department?

1167. Did your organization identify the full contract value and include options and provisions for renewals?

1168. Are required quality and service standards set?

1169. Is there a need for the procurement Assertive Community Treatment project at all?

1170. Is there a formal program of inservice training

for personnel in the business management function?

5.2 Contract Close-Out: Assertive Community Treatment

1171. Why Outsource?

1172. Have all contract records been included in the Assertive Community Treatment project archives?

1173. Have all acceptance criteria been met prior to final payment to contractors?

1174. Parties: who is involved?

1175. Change in attitude or behavior?

1176. What happens to the recipient of services?

1177. Parties: Authorized?

1178. Have all contracts been completed?

1179. Have all contracts been closed?

1180. Was the contract complete without requiring numerous changes and revisions?

1181. Change in circumstances?

1182. Change in knowledge?

1183. What is capture management?

1184. Has each contract been audited to verify

acceptance and delivery?

1185. How does it work?

1186. How is the contracting office notified of the automatic contract close-out?

1187. Are the signers the authorized officials?

1188. How/when used ?

1189. Was the contract type appropriate?

1190. Was the contract sufficiently clear so as not to result in numerous disputes and misunderstandings?

5.3 Project or Phase Close-Out: Assertive Community Treatment

1191. Complete yes or no?

1192. How often did each stakeholder need an update?

1193. If you were the Assertive Community Treatment project sponsor, how would you determine which Assertive Community Treatment project team(s) and/or individuals deserve recognition?

1194. What hierarchical authority does the stakeholder have in your organization?

1195. What could have been improved?

1196. What advantages do the an individual interview have over a group meeting, and vice-versa?

1197. Who exerted influence that has positively affected or negatively impacted the Assertive Community Treatment project?

1198. Can the lesson learned be replicated?

1199. What was expected from each stakeholder?

1200. Who are the Assertive Community Treatment project stakeholders and what are roles and involvement?

1201. Were the outcomes different from the already stated planned?

1202. Were messages directly related to the release strategy or phases of the Assertive Community Treatment project?

1203. What are the mandatory communication needs for each stakeholder?

1204. Have business partners been involved extensively, and what data was required for them?

1205. What was learned?

1206. In addition to assessing whether the Assertive Community Treatment project was successful, it is equally critical to analyze why it was or was not fully successful. Are you including this?

1207. What is a Risk Management Process?

1208. What are the informational communication needs for each stakeholder?

5.4 Lessons Learned: Assertive Community Treatment

1209. What is below the surface?

1210. What specialization does the task require?

1211. How will you allocate your funding resources?

1212. What is your overall assessment of the outcome of this Assertive Community Treatment project?

1213. How well does the product or service the Assertive Community Treatment project produced meet your needs?

1214. How extensive is middle management?

1215. To what extent was the evolution of risks communicated?

1216. How timely were Progress Reports provided to the Assertive Community Treatment project Manager by Team Members?

1217. What is the distribution of authority?

1218. How effective were the techniques used to prepare you and your organization for the impact of the changes brought about by the product or service produced by the Assertive Community Treatment project?

1219. How comprehensive was integration testing?

1220. What is the proportion of in-house and contractor personnel authorized for the Assertive Community Treatment project?

1221. What were the success factors?

1222. How to write up the lesson identified – how will you document the results of your analysis corresponding that you have an li ready to take the next step in the ll process?

1223. What is the frequency of communication?

1224. What were the most significant issues on this Assertive Community Treatment project?

1225. What are the performance measures?

1226. Who is responsible for each action?

1227. What other questions should you have asked?

1228. What regulatory regime controlled how your organization head and program manager directed your organization and Assertive Community Treatment project?

Index

CPSIA information can be obtained
at www.ICGtesting.com
Printed in the USA
LVHW011100230420
654319LV00002B/293

9 781867 306146